DIV

PRO

YOURSELF,

YOUR KIDS,

AND YOUR

FUTURE

D1315485

Section of Family Law Publications Development Board

DIVORCE: PROTECT YOURSELF, YOUR KIDS, AND YOUR FUTURE

RANDALL KESSLER

Printed in the United States of America.

18 17 16 15 14 5 4 3 2 1

Library of Congress Cataloging-in-Publication Data

Library of Congress Cataloging-in-Publication Data

Kessler, Randall M., author.
  Divorce : protect yourself, your kids, and your future / Randall M. Kessler, Esq.
    pages cm
  ISBN 978-1-62722-573-1 (alk. paper)
  1. Divorce--Law and legislation--United States--Popular works. I. American Bar Association. Section of Family Law, sponsoring body. II. Title.
  KF535.Z9.K47 2014
  346.7301'66--dc23
                                        2014006154

Discounts are available for books ordered in bulk. Special consideration is given to state bars, CLE programs, and other bar-related organizations. Inquire at Book Publishing, ABA Publishing, American Bar Association, 321 N. Clark Street, Chicago, Illinois 60654-7598.

www.ShopABA.org

This book is dedicated to everyone who has ever faced or may face a divorce. It can be such a frightening experience. I hope this book gives you reassurance you can survive the process and have a wonderful life again. It may take time, but if you persevere, you will find joy and laughter and look back on your divorce as a test you successfully passed.

Life is full of challenges. I wish you success in them. And most of all, that you find love and cherish it. It is out there, waiting for you to find it again.

Go get it.

Contents

Chapter 7
Child Support

Preface

My name is Randy Kessler and I have been a divorce lawyer for more than 25 years. As the founding partner of Kessler & Solomiany, LLC, I have represented some of the most famous people in the world, including world-class athletes, the business elite, music moguls, and blockbuster entertainers. However, for the majority of my career, my primary focus has been on people like you—the everyday husband or wife who feels lost and confused.

Regardless of where you fall on this spectrum, my goal always is the same—to serve each individual with the highest degree of integrity, helping to rebuild strong lives and return hope where it once appeared to be lost forever. Yes, I am a divorce lawyer, but I prefer to call myself a family lawyer, someone who can help return freedom, peace, and predictability to deserving spouses and families. I look forward to a day when my services will no longer be in high demand; until that day, however, I can only give you my assurances that there is hope, and that your feelings of confusion, anger, sadness, and loss are temporary.

Divorce: Protect Yourself, Your Kids, and Your Future was written to help you prepare yourself for what may be the most important business and personal transaction of the rest of your life. I wrote this book with the everyday individual in mind, someone just like you—not someone with a law degree. Almost every day I see clients in my office who have many of the same concerns, misconceptions, and questions about the often confusing and complicated divorce process you may be experiencing. In the coming pages, I will show you, step by step, how to select an attorney, ask the right questions to help get the crucial answers you need, prepare for trial, and much more.

Please note that the terms *attorney* and *lawyer* mean the same thing, so do not be confused if you hear or read one or the other and do not know if there is a difference. For purposes of this book, the terms are used interchangeably.

Introduction

You have arrived at a decision: you want a divorce or you are seriously thinking about it. Or perhaps your spouse has made that decision for you, and now you are forced to think about how to protect yourself. Regardless of who initiated it, the decision to divorce is rarely a sudden one. Perhaps when you look in the mirror each morning you say to yourself, "I need to get out of this marriage. It is no longer working and it is beyond repair. I need to start a new life." Or maybe your spouse has made that decision. We all want to stay in love forever, but that is not always life's reality. Nearly 50 percent of all marriages in the United States will end in divorce. Nobody wants to be part of this statistic, but when all hope for reconciliation is gone, sometimes divorce is the only avenue for recapturing the life you deserve.

Divorce is stressful and can be a painful process for everyone involved, including your soon-to-be former spouse, your family, and your children. The decision should not be made without serious consideration. Reading this book will not make your divorce easy, nor will it convince you that you should or shouldn't get a divorce if you are not sure. However, if you or your spouse has made the tough decision to go ahead with a divorce, welcome to step one.

This book results from more than 25 years of practical experience and application. I have been practicing family law in Atlanta, Georgia, since June 1988. After graduating from Brandeis University near Boston and Emory University School of Law in Atlanta, I created a family law firm in downtown Atlanta. Our firm has a team of more than 25 professionals, including lawyers, paralegals, and clerks, making Kessler & Solomiany, LLC, one of the largest and most prominent family law firms in the Southeast. Apart from my role as founding partner of Kessler & Solomiany, LLC, I am also active in the local and national legal communities. In 2011, I was elected chair of the Family Law Sections of the American Bar Association and of the State Bar of Georgia.

Prior to becoming the chair of the Family Law Section of the American Bar Association, I served the bar and the public in many ways, including as chair of the Family Law Section of the Atlanta Bar Association, as editor of the State Bar of Georgia's Family Law Review, as a guest instructor at Emory University School of Law (teaching trial techniques), and as an adjunct professor at John Marshall Law School in Atlanta (teaching family law). I am truly fortunate and grateful to be in a position to help others.

In my more than 25 years of practicing family law, I have been involved in almost every type of case. I have experienced many different divorce and custody matters. What I discuss in this book results from actual outcomes from countless cases I have tried. These cases involved real, ordinary people just like you—not just the celebrities you see on television or in the tabloids. My clients are often people who tried therapy and marital counseling without success and attempted to salvage a relationship that no longer worked for either person. They are people, like you, who made the tough decision to seek a divorce for the health and welfare of themselves and their families.

Despite their differences with their former spouses, many clients agreed on emotionally charged issues such as, Who gets to stay in the house? Who gets the car? What happens to the family business? And, most important, where will the kids live and when will they see the other parent? I fought hard for my clients—their concerns became my concerns—and I cared about each of them during their case and was invested in what would happen to them after their divorce became final.

You owe it to yourself and your family to be fully prepared. This book offers meaningful and clear guidance on what to expect during every step of a divorce. These steps include finding a lawyer, developing a budget, filing and serving divorce papers, determining costs, taking deposition testimony, seeking custody of children, and dividing assets. *Divorce: Protect Yourself, Your Kids, and Your Future* is your basic road map for getting a divorce in America today. However, before proceeding, understand that no two divorces are alike and divorce laws vary from state to state. This book cannot and should not be a substitute for legal advice from a lawyer qualified to represent you in your city and state. This book will answer many of your questions and prepare you to ask the right questions as you proceed through this complex and emotional endeavor.

If you are ready to look forward and construct a new life for yourself, then the two most important steps for making this happen are (1) to meet with a lawyer and (2) to get informed. Only you can take the first step. *Divorce: Protect Yourself, Your Kids, and Your Future* is your personal guidebook for taking the second step. It is meant to be an easy-to-understand resource to assist you in navigating the overwhelming process of divorce. Hopefully this book will make a positive difference in your and your family's journey. I am dedicated to helping every client feel safe and secure and to supporting clients as they move through life with courage and knowledge, creating the outcomes and futures they and you desire and deserve.

Chapter 1

The First Step: Find the Right Lawyer

Divorce. It is a striking and dramatic word that conjures up endless questions. How does it really happen? Will I have to stand opposite my spouse detailing the awful breakdown of our sex life and personal issues in front of strangers? How can I determine what property I will end up with when this is all over? What will my life look like after the divorce? How often will I be able to see my children?

The emotional, mental, and psychological confusion of divorce creates many more questions. This book will help answer them, including how and where to get started.

1. Should I talk to a lawyer?

Yes. If you can afford a lawyer, then schedule an initial consultation. You need to discuss your circumstances as soon as possible. Don't just call a family friend who happens to be a lawyer or find someone online; contact an attorney who specializes in divorce and/or family law. The Constitution of the United States grants the states the power to regulate issues relating to the family. Therefore, each state's divorce laws are different and only a trained family law attorney in your state knows your state's laws. Remember, your lawyer is there to protect your interests throughout what may be a long and complicated ordeal, and that can occur only if he or she understands the intricacies of divorce law in your state.

Even if you are parting with your spouse as friends and think you can handle the division of your property and other matters on your own, don't be naïve. Although you were once a union of two people, you are becoming two individuals again. Sadly, even the closest friends can disagree on the division of money, property, and goods, as well as issues relating to their children. Your spouse will get a lawyer, so you should as well, even if you think it is an amicable divorce. And no, one lawyer cannot represent both of you, as that is an ethical conflict for the lawyer. You need a lawyer who is 100 percent on your side with no divided loyalties.

Be aware, getting a divorce in America today is not like appearing in a courtroom on reality television. It will not be neatly wrapped up in a 30-minute time slot. The process can last months or even years, with lengthy negotiations over the division of property and money, custody, and any other issues that come up. Finding a lawyer you can trust and depend on will help you navigate the most expeditious course through these swirling waters.

2. Is what I tell my lawyer private?

When you get a divorce, your lawyer becomes your newest confidante—however, not in the way your siblings or best friend from college are confidantes. What you tell your lawyer is legally privileged. Your attorney owes you the duty of confidentiality. Except in limited circumstances (if a crime is about to be committed or a child has been abused), your attorney cannot—and will not—disclose the information you give him or her to a third party. This duty of confidentiality even extends into pretrial and trial disclosure of information obtained from you in confidence. If the court or an opposing party requests this information, your attorney will decline the request, citing the attorney-client privilege, an evidentiary privilege that makes information obtained by the attorney in the course of legal representation inadmissible in court. Attorneys take this duty of confidentiality very seriously and are obligated to maintain the information in confidence. Ask your lawyer about this.

You need to be completely honest with your lawyer and understand that the information you give him or her will not be made public, with the exceptions mentioned previously. It is usually better to admit you once committed a crime (or exercise the right against self-incrimination) than to lie about it under oath. Think about the Martha Stewart case. If she had not lied about and tried to cover up what she did, she might not have been jailed. You and your lawyer may need to discuss how to present certain problematic evidence, but your lawyer will tell you not to lie under oath. If you tell your lawyer a fact and later deny it under oath, your attorney will maintain his or her duty of confidentiality but will likely have to withdraw from representing you in your case.

3. Should I talk to a lawyer to find out if I want to get a divorce?

Your desire to end your marriage cannot—and should not—be determined by an attorney. It can be determined only by you or your spouse. The fact that you are looking for a divorce lawyer may mean you or your spouse has already determined your marriage is over. Many people who walk into divorce attorneys' offices do not have one specific reason they want to get a divorce. For many, it is a culmination of months or years of frustration, anger, and sadness. For others, it may be a sudden realization that the marriage is over, often due to infidelity. What all these people have in common is they know divorce is the step they need to take.

Your attorney is focused on trying to help you through this tough process—the divorce. He or she will help you examine the facts of your case and give you an informed and honest opinion about what you can expect to receive in a divorce: a share of your marital assets, custody of your children, support payments (child support or alimony), and many other aspects. A lawyer may tell you that in your state, judges are unlikely to grant ownership of a house to a spouse who has already vacated the premises to move into an apartment with his or her new girlfriend or boyfriend. However, a lawyer will not look into your eyes and say, "You do not really want to get a divorce. You are still in love with your spouse. Give it one more chance." If you want to hear marital advice, consult a marriage counselor or your best friend. If you want to know if you can expect a judge to divide your spouse's stock assets and give you an equitable portion, talk to an attorney.

It is your marriage. It is your divorce. And it is your life. Only you (or your spouse) can decide to get a divorce. While you should be able to confide in your attorney about your feelings and the unpleasant experiences you have endured, do not turn your attorney into your best friend or marriage counselor. Let the attorney handle the custody and financial issues. Turn to your friends, family, and perhaps a therapist to work on emotional issues.

4. What kind of person should my divorce lawyer be?

Here is a list, by no means exhaustive, of important qualities your lawyer should possess. He or she should be someone who:

- gives you the confidence to talk candidly,
- listens when you have something to say,
- makes you feel comfortable about the divorce process,
- is willing to answer any questions, and
- discusses (on your first visit) the costs associated with your case, including fees for legal services and the costs of each procedure.

The characteristics highlighted above focus on one basic principle: At the heart of every attorney-client relationship there must be complete disclosure of confidential and often embarrassing information. Complete disclosure will occur only if you feel comfortable with the person you choose to be your attorney. Nothing good can come from having a misinformed lawyer or you misunderstanding the consequences of an action. Divorce costs can be significant, even for a case that is only somewhat contested. An attorney who will not tell you his or her fees up front is not someone you want to have representing you in this process.

The decision about whom to hire is yours. Hire a lawyer you feel comfortable with and who you believe will provide the best representation. You may identify more with an attorney of your own gender; you may prefer someone of the opposite gender who you think may better predict your spouse's emotional responses; you may want the most expensive, experienced attorney in your state because you have many contested issues or, alternatively, you may want a more low-key attorney, with a modest office you do not find intimidating. The choice is yours for whatever reason you decide.

Regardless of whom you ultimately choose, it is understandable that you will feel some apprehension when you first walk into the lawyer's office. This is a new process and you are likely experiencing significant stress, which is only magnified by the fact that you do not know the attorney or the staff. However, the right lawyer will quickly put those apprehensions to rest.

5. How do I find a divorce lawyer (or family law attorney)?

If you live in a relatively populous area, you should be able to locate a published list of family law attorneys in your vicinity. You can look in the printed telephone or online directories and start cold-calling attorneys who advertise their divorce services. However, this probably is not the best method and it is not recommended.

Instead, try calling your state's bar association office. *Bar* is a word that refers to the practice of law. Practicing law is a licensed profession, so an attorney must have a valid license to practice. Most state (and city) bar associations will have referral services of divorce lawyers in your area. There are also national guidebooks provided by companies such as Martindale-Hubbell and FindLaw. These comprehensive listings of attorneys in your area who specialize in family law can be found at your local public library or on the Internet at www.martindale.com, www.lawyers.com, or www.findlaw.com. There are also websites such as www.avvo.com, www.superlawyers.com, or other similar services that list and may also rate attorneys as well.

However, the best kind of referral comes from someone you trust. Talk to someone who has dealt with a divorce attorney and ask him or her about the experience. When you ask your friends, family, and co-workers for advice, speak to them in confidence. Although it may be hard and even embarrassing to ask for their help, remember that this is probably one of the most important business and personal transactions you will ever make and the outcome could determine your children's well-being, your financial security, and your happiness. Another option is to ask an attorney you or your friends know and respect (who may not be a divorce attorney) whom they would suggest. Even lawyers who do not practice family law know who the well-respected family law attorneys are.

After you have received a list of potential attorneys, if possible, call and schedule an initial interview, also known as a consultation. Interview more than one attorney during this initial stage. Also, remember that any information you share during these initial interviews will not be disclosed by the attorney to any third party—including your spouse, friends, or family. Expect to pay for these consultations. Ask each attorney about the fee when you call for the appointment. Although multiple consultations may be cost-prohibitive for some, if you can afford this expense, it is well worth it. And no, if you have a consultation with an attorney, your spouse may not consult with or hire that attorney, even if you don't ultimately hire him or her.

6. What if I use a family friend or a general practitioner for an uncontested divorce?

If you are truly in a situation where there is little or no money to be divided, everyone gets along, and you just want a piece of paper that says you are divorced, a close friend or family attorney may be fine. He or she can file the appropriate papers and the whole matter may take only a few months. Even then there may be issues a seasoned family attorney would understand that a nonfamily law attorney would not, but again, the cost may be prohibitive.

Most people are not in an easy, agreeable situation. They disagree over how much money and property each person will receive, who will take ownership of the house, and who will get the kids and the family pets. Remember, if you have something to fight about—or if there is enough money in the estate that there could be a potential conflict—the first thing to do is call a divorce lawyer.

Even if you are confident that you and your spouse can come to an amicable settlement, divorce law is very complicated and even an uncontested divorce can take a turn for the worse. Also, be mindful there are many personal details your lawyer must know. You may not be comfortable discussing your extramarital affairs with a lawyer who is also your father's best army buddy. Even though the lawyer is sworn to secrecy, your comfort level is key. The best recommendation is to find an attorney who is outside of your immediate circle of friends and family and who handles only or mostly divorce cases.

If you live in a small town or rural area where there may be only a few attorneys practicing, it might be impossible to consult a full-time family lawyer. In such situations, your best bet would be to consult your local general practice lawyer, as this person will be familiar with the local court system. However, if you need a more specialized attorney with experience in divorce or custody cases, travel to the nearest large city or find a divorce specialist willing to travel to your location to work with you.

7. What is an initial consultation?

An initial consultation is exactly what it sounds like—it is the first discussion with your lawyer (or potential lawyer, as you may not hire the first lawyer you interview) about your case. The initial consultation may take an hour or more. At the outset, be prepared to give a detailed version of the facts that led you to consider divorce, and be completely honest. Do not lie to your lawyer or neglect to inform him or her about important details because you are embarrassed or fear you will be judged. Tell your lawyer all the details of your situation, including adulterous relationships, violent behavior, lying, financial misdeeds, and substance abuse. Your lawyer will appreciate your candor and recognize you are putting your life in his or her hands. Remember, while this process may be new to you, your lawyer has heard just about every possible reason for divorce imaginable.

The initial consultation is your first opportunity to discuss your case with your lawyer: what you want, what you don't want, and your expectations. It is also your lawyer's opportunity to explain to you his or her recommended course of action, applicable defenses, and what you can expect through the divorce process. Tell your lawyer all of the facts and listen to what he or she says about your case, as that is the only way you can decide if this is the right lawyer to represent you. Also remember that anything you divulge to your attorney during your initial consultation will remain private.

8. What questions should I ask myself during the initial consultation?

The initial consultation is your first—and sometimes only—opportunity to size up your prospective attorney. During and after your initial consult you should ask yourself the following questions to determine whether the lawyer you are about to select is right for you.

Does this lawyer listen to me, or does he or she just talk and lecture?

One key to a successful attorney-client relationship is that each party is informed. Your attorney will likely be well versed in the law in your particular jurisdiction. However, he or she will not be familiar with your particular circumstances and how the law applies to them. Conversely, you will likely be unfamiliar with the law, but your personal knowledge of your own life is invaluable. Therefore, both you and the attorney must be willing and able to communicate this information to each other for you to receive effective representation. Your stress level is likely to increase, not lessen, during the divorce process, so finding a lawyer who will listen to your concerns is important.

Is this a lawyer who primarily handles divorce cases?

There are many nuances in a divorce proceeding, and therefore it is important for your lawyer to be familiar with every option. Just like physicians, lawyers specialize. You would not want to see an ophthalmologist for a sprained ankle, so why would you want to hire a tax attorney to handle your divorce?

Is this attorney someone with whom I feel comfortable?

This cannot be stressed enough. You may have to discuss intimate details of your life because your lawyer must be informed to be fully prepared for every situation. This will occur only if you feel your attorney is trustworthy and sincere about helping you through this trying time.

Can I afford this attorney's services?

Again, a lawyer should be up front about fee structures when you call for an initial appointment. If the cost of retaining this person's services is unclear, ask for clarification. Don't be afraid to ask about various fee options at the beginning of the process. There will probably be a charge for the initial consultation; however, fees will vary depending on the attorney's expertise and status in the legal community, and some attorneys offer free initial consultations.

9. What documents should I bring to the initial consultation?

In most states, you will be required to fill out a domestic relations financial affidavit (DRFA) or something similar. The DRFA is a sworn statement attesting to your income, assets, debts, liabilities, monthly expenses, and any other relevant financial information. If you go to court later on, the judge will not want to whip out a calculator to add up your monthly water, gas, and grocery bills. Instead, he or she will want to know how much money you need to live and how much you earn each month. Provide that information accurately. If you are not comfortable preparing this statement, enlist the help of a certified public accountant or ask your attorney for a recommendation on how to proceed.

Your DRFA may become the most important document in your case. Take your time and make it accurate. Be honest. Go over all of your expenses and work with your attorney to make sure you are not leaving anything important out of your list of needs. Do not feel guilty or greedy; this is not the time to be conservative and show the judge how thrifty you can be. No one will be impressed—including the judge. Do not lie or exaggerate either. If you spend a lot of money on jewelry or other luxuries, put that expense in the affidavit, but do not include expenses that are on your wish list.

This DRFA may be the first document you complete in your divorce process and, to repeat, it may also be the most important. Your attorney may be required to send this to the court early in the process so the court and opposing counsel know of your immediate expense needs. A judge may use your DRFA later on to determine how much money you will receive to live on.

Remember that despite the adversarial nature of divorce, your attorney and the court require full disclosure. Two households now must live on the same finances that previously supported only one household. This means you may not receive all the relief you seek; however, if you do not ask for it, you will definitely not get it. Finding a balance is the key, which is one of the most important things to realize and come to terms with in your divorce.

10. Should I create a chronology of my marriage for the initial consultation?

A written chronology of your marriage and the events that led up to you seeking a divorce can be invaluable to your attorney and the court. A chronology sums up the important dates and events of your marriage for your lawyer to use as a guideline. Your attorney may have literally dozens of clients; therefore, he or she probably cannot remember and state the facts of your case completely from memory. By writing out a timeline of your marriage, you can provide your lawyer with something concrete to refer to before a deposition, mediation, or trial. Your attorney can also look at his or her notes and the letters and documents you provided, but the most important reference is your own chronology. It costs nothing to prepare—except a little of your time—and often the process can be therapeutic for you.

11. When should I ask about what it all may cost?

Right away! You are hiring a highly skilled professional to steer you through a major financial and personal undertaking. Would you schedule a remodeling of your home without asking how much it will cost? Of course not—you would receive documentation about every step in the procedure. A divorce is no different. There is no real way to predict what will happen, how long it may take, how the other party will react, or how much money will be at stake, but your attorney can discuss all the options and variables and give you a ballpark estimate of the costs.

Attorneys' fees vary from state to state, from city to city, and in different-sized communities, and are usually charged by the hour. Some attorneys charge a set fee for an initial consultation, which may last for an hour or more, or they may charge by the hour. The range of consultation and hourly fees can be from $50 up to $1,000 or more. Some attorneys may offer unbundled services or limited representation terms that are based on handling a portion of a case, whether drafting a document, preparing you for a deposition or testimony at trial, or explaining the terms of a child custody plan. Ask what the minimum time charge is (0.1, 0.2, or 0.25), how and if they use their staff (what paralegal or assistant time charges may apply), and what expenses you will be responsible for (copies, postage, fax charges, etc.). Lawyers should be open to such questions.

When you hire a divorce attorney, he or she will usually request that you pay an initial retainer fee. This fee is paid to the lawyer to secure the firm's services for your divorce proceeding and to guarantee payment of fees, and it may or may not be refundable. Retainer fees vary depending on the complexity of your case. The more complicated your case, the higher the retainer. Expect to replenish your initial retainer if it is depleted during your case. If an attorney charges $200 per hour, your initial $5,000 retainer will be depleted after 25 hours of work by the attorney and his or her staff—including research, trial prep, day-long depositions, and trial. Hearing the prices up front may be a shock. It is a good sign if an attorney is honest about the costs. You would not want to have that shock as your divorce is finalized and you get the bill!

By now you should have a better understanding of how and why to hire a lawyer to guide you through this complicated process. When you have found a lawyer with whom you feel comfortable, what do you do to get started? As has been mentioned, the first step should be an initial consultation. In the next chapter, we will look at the nuances of this very important first phase so you are better positioned to begin your divorce.

12. How do I know how much is reasonable for my attorney to charge?

A lawyer who charges high fees or has a fancy office may not be the best lawyer for you and your case. As with hiring any professional, the key is learning about the lawyer's experience and credentials. A lawyer's track record and reputation are critical. You will also need to look at your budget and figure out how much you can afford to spend in legal fees. The American Bar Association's Model Rules of Professional Responsibility—which many states' bar associations base their own rules of professional conduct upon—states in Rule 1.5(a) that a lawyer shall not charge an unreasonable fee for his or her services. Rule 1.5(a) lists eight factors that should be considered in determining whether a fee is reasonable:

- the time and labor required, the novelty and difficulty of the questions involved, and the skill requisite to perform the legal service properly;
- the likelihood, if apparent to the client, that the acceptance of the employment will preclude other employment by the lawyer;
- the fee customarily charged in the locality for similar legal services;
- the amount involved and the results obtained;
- the time limitations imposed by the client or by the circumstances;
- the nature and length of the professional relationship with the client;
- the experience, reputation, and ability of the lawyer or lawyers performing the services; and
- whether the fee is fixed or contingent.

It is also important to note that Rule 1.5(a), Section D of the Model Rules of Professional Responsibility prohibits an attorney from entering into an agreement in any domestic relations matter if payment is contingent upon securing a divorce or upon the alimony, support, or property settlement. See Model Rules of Professional Responsibility, Rule 1.5(a)(d) (accessible at www.abanet.org/cpr/mrpc/rule_1_5.html). Divorce lawyers are prohibited from getting a percentage of the settlement as their fee in a divorce.

The factors mentioned above illustrate that a high-priced lawyer is not necessarily better, but generally, the best divorce lawyers charge more because their experience and results allow them to do so. However, if your case is simple and does not involve a large sum of money to fight over, a high-priced attorney may not be best for your needs. Many law firms will have associates and paralegals who can also work with you on certain aspects of your case or answer questions. Your lawyer should have a support staff of paralegals, administrative assistants, and fellow attorneys that can aid him or her in managing the workload. These professionals will charge a lower fee for their services, reducing your total cost.

The most important thing is that you feel confident in your lawyer's ability to handle your case competently. Talk to your lawyer. Get a sense that he or she is listening to you and addressing the specific needs of your case, not just telling you what he or she tells everyone who walks in the door. It is important to have an experienced attorney who will look at your case with an open mind and who will to listen to your concerns. You are hiring a professional. As the client, you have rights and privileges. You have the right to ask questions. You have the right to understand every step you and your attorney take in this process. You have the right to say no if you do not approve of a tactic. Make sure you are comfortable with your choice of lawyer.

Chapter 2

Before You File for Divorce: Preliminary Decisions

You have pored over the names and references given to you by your closest friends and family, checked them out on the Internet, and selected the lawyer you believe is best suited to help you through this tough process. Now you must begin to communicate the important details of your case to your lawyer and make some important decisions that may affect what your postdivorce life looks like. This will require a great deal of information and documents your lawyer will need at the onset of your representation. This information and exchange of documents will occur early on, perhaps at your initial meeting or right after you have hired your attorney. From there your attorney will be better situated to help you make the important preliminary decisions that may affect your postdivorce life.

1. Do I need to have a ground for getting a divorce?

You may have heard terms such as *irreconcilable differences*, *mental cruelty*, and *adultery* in reference to grounds for divorce. The term *ground* refers to the reason you are seeking this legal dissolution of your marriage. In most states, there are multiple grounds for divorce.

One ground each state offers is "no-fault," meaning there does not need to be a showing of wrongdoing by either party. The fact that one party considers the marriage irrevocably broken means that a divorce can take place. No-fault divorces are available in all 50 states (although laws may change, so talk to a lawyer in your state). Most divorces are granted on such grounds, even though other grounds may exist.

There are also fault-based grounds for seeking a divorce. These could include mental cruelty or adultery, but more and more, courts are not basing the divorce on these grounds. Sometimes a person is determined to receive a divorce because of the adultery of the other spouse, and some judges may grant the divorce based on this claim. However, usually the judge or your attorney will ask during direct or cross-examination, "Do you believe that this marriage is beyond repair?" If the answer is yes, then that may be all a judge must know to grant the divorce. Adultery, abuse, and other conduct issues may still be vital components of your case and affect other decisions the court must make. For example, in some states adultery may be a complete bar to alimony, and child or spousal abuse will affect the court's custody determination, but not whether the marriage will be dissolved.

2. What magnitude does adultery have in a divorce proceeding?

Often, it affects little; forget what you have seen on *Divorce Court* reruns regarding adultery. In most states, the court will not grant you extra money because of your spouse's adulterous affair. However, in some states, adultery may affect the court's decision on alimony and property division. Adultery may also play into the court's determination of how to award parenting time with the children. But more important than the mere presence of adultery is how it took place (for example, were the children in the next room?) and how that may demonstrate a parent's poor judgment. Consult an attorney in your jurisdiction for legal advice regarding the consequences of an adulterous relationship.

3. What are some other grounds for divorce?

Since the court needs to determine only that the marriage is over to grant the divorce, grounds for divorce are not as important as they used to be. Grounds for divorce and conduct issues a court may look at, other than adultery, are spousal abuse, drug and alcohol abuse, and abandonment, meaning leaving a spouse for a long period of time with no support given. While they are rarely used for the divorce itself, these issues can be raised to show the court why it is inequitable or unfair for one spouse to receive, or not to receive, certain property or alimony and are often very relevant to custody and visitation decisions.

4. Should I move out of the house and get an apartment?

Whether to move out of the marital residence is a question you should discuss with your attorney during the initial meeting or soon after. Deciding when and how to move out of the home you have been living in with your spouse is up to you, but there are important factors you must consider prior to making your decision. Do you hope to gain ownership of the house in the divorce? Do you hope to live there when your divorce is final? Judges are human. Like most people, they are unlikely to change something that seems to be working.

They want to maintain the status quo. If you want to eventually live in and receive ownership of the marital estate, stay in the house as long as possible (unless, of course, there is domestic violence). Know that many states require a period of separation without cohabitation. Staying in your marital home might not violate this rule if you do not have sexual relations with your spouse and perhaps sleep in different rooms. Consult an attorney in your state regarding your decision to stay in the marital home.

When cohabitation is possible, often it is best to let the judge be the one to remove you or your spouse from the house, unless your spouse will voluntarily move out, but that will be a decision you'll need to make after discussing the situation fully with your lawyer. At the end of your divorce, the judge may not want to rearrange everyone's lives—especially if children are involved. If you move into an apartment and your spouse is living in the house, the judge may think, "This person seems to be taking good care of the house and the children seem to be adjusting well. I guess that spouse should retain ownership." Your goal right now is to set up the life situation you hope to maintain after the divorce. If you want the house, continue to live there. If you want full custody of your kids, within reason, remain living with them. But know that judges dislike parents who keep children from other parents, so unless there are very good reasons your spouse should not get quality time with the children, you should do what is in your children's best interests. In cases of spousal abuse, continuing to live together may be impossible. If there is violence or potential harm, you should never put yourself or your children in a dangerous or vulnerable situation. Always call 911 if violence occurs.

5. What is legal separation?

The definition of legal separation varies from state to state, but typically it means that a husband and wife are no longer having sexual relations and consider themselves separated. They may or may not be residing apart. In some states you do not need a court to grant a legal separation. In others it is a cause of action in which the parties continue to be married but there is a court order granting them a legal separation and determining issues of property division, support (both spousal and child), custody, and any other issues the court could decide in a divorce.

6. Can I get temporary support for my kids and me during my separation?

Talk to your attorney immediately and explain that you are responsible for the care of your children and you need to work out an arrangement with your spouse about monthly expenses. Do not assume that your estranged spouse will be flexible and understanding just because it involves the children you both love. A divorce involves highly charged emotions, and sometimes, although it is tragic, children can be caught in the conflict. That is why all states have specific rules and guidelines concerning child support. Ask your attorney if he or she has these statutes prepared in an easy-to-understand document. You can reach a temporary arrangement to cover your and your children's needs, either by agreement or by court intervention. But yes, you should be able to get temporary support during your separation.

7. Should I keep my plans for divorce secret from my spouse for now?

Talk to a lawyer before talking to your spouse about divorce. One of the hardest transformations for a person is to go from "husband and wife" to "husband versus wife." Mostly, you have been working and thinking as a couple. Nevertheless, think about yourself and what is best for you as an individual. This point bears repeating—you are becoming an individual and you must protect yourself.

It may be difficult to think this way. You may still have deep feelings for your spouse, complicated by anger, love, guilt, depression, or confusion. However, once you decide to divorce, or once your spouse makes that decision, your identity as a couple transforms into two individual identities. A divorce is an individual process and your lawyer can represent only you and your interests. Your spouse will get a lawyer to represent his or her own interests. Do not be naïve and believe your spouse and his or her lawyer will be looking out for your best interest when it comes time to discuss the division of property and money and child custody.

Divorce can be an adversarial process; therefore, if you prepare documents and financial affidavits before you approach your spouse about getting a divorce, keep these documents in a place where you are sure your spouse will not find them. Be absolutely sure! You may wish to purchase a new safe deposit box (not the one you share but he or she never goes into—there's always a first time). You may store the papers with a trusted relative or friend, someone you feel confident will keep your plans a secret. Get a new, safe, private e-mail account with a safe password and secret questions your spouse will not easily guess.

Remember that once you reveal your intentions to someone, even your mother or oldest school friend, the secret is shared. Even a loving parent firmly on your side may slip up and talk about your impending divorce with others. Be prepared to have your spouse discover your intentions before you are ready to confront him or her with them. If you want to maintain complete secrecy for a while, tell nobody, except perhaps a therapist whom you do not share with your spouse and who must maintain your confidence—until you are ready to file for divorce and serve your spouse with divorce papers. Your family and friends will understand that divorce is a sensitive matter and one of the most personal decisions anyone can make.

8. What are the first documents filed?

Your attorney will draft and file your petition for divorce, detailing for the court the reasons you are entitled to a divorce and what you are asking for, such as custody, alimony, and property division. You and your lawyer will review the documents carefully to ensure they are accurate. Once you authorize your attorney to file them, you will have begun litigation, a divorce lawsuit will be pending, and you will be in a contested divorce until settlement of all issues is reached.

These divorce papers will then be served (delivered) to your spouse. The question of how to serve your spouse, how to give him or her proper legal notice that the case has been filed, is a very serious one that requires much thought. You will be viewed by your spouse as sending a message. The question is, do you want that message sent by sheriff, private detective, or letter? There are many other variables to consider concerning the difficulty of getting the documents to your spouse. If your spouse already has a lawyer, serving him or her should be much easier as most lawyers will have their client accept service by signing a document either lawyer prepares indicating that the recipient is aware of the lawsuit.

After the petition for divorce has been served, the recipient and his or her lawyer will prepare the answer, the document containing the response to the divorce petition. It sets forth what the parties agree upon and what they do not agree upon. For instance, the parties will usually agree that they are married and live in a certain county and state. They may even agree there is a custody dispute. But they may indicate they disagree about things as well, such as whether any premarital property exists. The contents of the answer will depend on what is written in the petition. Often contained within the answer is a counterclaim or countersuit for divorce indicating the defendant is also suing for divorce.

Once these preliminary tasks are completed, you will be in the pretrial phase of your case. This is the phase of your divorce in which you and your spouse will be asked to exchange information and possibly be deposed, or questioned, under oath by opposing counsel about specific facts of your case. In the next chapter, we will discuss what you can expect during your deposition and what documents can be requested.

Chapter 3

The Pretrial Stage: Discovery and the Deposition

You have picked your attorney, disclosed every relevant aspect of your life to him or her, and filed for divorce. Or perhaps your spouse filed for divorce and served you with divorce papers. You are now in the pretrial stage of your divorce, the time between filing and your final trial. For the next few months you and your attorney will be involved in the discovery process, a period of time during which you must provide the opposing party with all relevant tangible documents, such as tax returns, as well as your own oral testimony. As information becomes available to both parties, your attorney may—at your or the court's direction—try to mediate a settlement, hoping to avoid a final trial.

In the coming chapters we will discuss what you can expect from a deposition, mediation as an alternative to trial, and hearings to determine important matters such as temporary child custody and spousal support until the final trial. For now, let's turn to discovery and the deposition process.

1. What is discovery?

Before the court or the parties can make an informed decision about how to divide the marital assets in a divorce, there should be a meticulous accounting of those assets, which is done through a process called discovery. Discovery is a somewhat informal method—usually performed between the attorneys and parties themselves—whereby the litigants exchange important financial information and documents, answer questions under oath during a deposition, and admit or deny in writing allegations posed by the spouse's attorney. The discovery phase of your case takes place after the petition for divorce and an answer by the opposing party have been filed.

The purpose of discovery is for each side to obtain nonprivileged information that can be useful for an informed defense without requiring court intervention and expensive litigation fees. In this chapter you will get an understanding of the discovery methods that attorneys use, including interrogatories, requests for production of documents, requests for admissions, and depositions.

2. Why should I voluntarily disclose information?

Yes, the American legal system is adversarial. However, one of the fundamental building blocks of our system is that in a court of law all parties must be on an equal playing field. Theoretically, this can occur only when both parties are fully informed of the evidence against them and any other information that will be detrimental or helpful to their case. This is probably not what you are used to seeing on television, where attorneys call surprise witnesses or parties blurt out confessions in open court. In actuality, attorneys are usually well aware of who will be called to testify against their client and exactly what those witnesses will say because they have already been deposed (questioned under oath) and served with interrogatories, requests for production of documents, and requests for admissions. And, perhaps most important, if the parties do not voluntarily share information, the court can be asked to make them do so and to pay the costs incurred in requesting the court's involvement as well.

3. What is an interrogatory?

Interrogatories are written questions that one party asks the other party to answer under oath. Interrogatories will flesh out details that may be relevant to a party's case or defense. If your spouse makes a lot of money, for example, but you are not sure where that money comes from—salary, stocks, real estate, and so on—you may send interrogatories asking, "Please state the account number for each bank account you own either jointly or separately." Or perhaps you expect your spouse will accuse you of being a bad parent. If so, then your interrogatory may ask, "Please state with specificity all of the complaints or concerns you have with your spouse's parenting." Maybe you suspect your spouse has been cheating on you, which may affect property division and an alimony award. Your interrogatory could ask, "Please give a list of names and contact information of anyone with whom you have had sexual intercourse outside of your marriage."

As you can see, the possibilities are almost endless, making interrogatories a useful tool to discover relevant and unprivileged information at this early stage of litigation. Yes, people lie on their responses to interrogatories, but the responses must be sworn to, so a lie on a response is tantamount to perjury. And again, if someone lies and is caught, that is often much more damaging to his or her case than a truthful answer would have been, even if the truthful answer disclosed misconduct. Lying forfeits your credibility.

you were in court. In court, the relevance would be determined by the judge. However, in a deposition, which is meant to gather important facts in the case, a lawyer can ask witnesses questions that may lead to relevant or admissible information. The questioning you will face at a deposition is broader than what you will face at trial.

Remember that you must answer every question you are asked at the deposition. Your attorney is well trained to object to any question he or she believes is beyond the scope of the divorce proceeding or involves privileged information, such as details protected by attorney-client privilege, as discussed in Chapter 1. Your attorney's objection will be on the record, so the judge can make a ruling after the deposition as to the propriety of a given question. In some circumstances, your lawyer may advise you not to answer a question; however, unless you are given this instruction, you should answer every question honestly, even if the answer is simply "I don't know."

Below is a guide to help you have a successful deposition:

- *Say no more!* Here is a game to test your ability to answer the question asked: If an attorney asked you, "Do you know what time it is?" what would be your response? Most people would respond, "It is 7:30 p.m." Is this the right answer? No! You did not answer the question you were asked. You inferred that the person asking if you knew what time it was wanted to know the actual time. However, the lawyer asked you if you knew the time. The correct answer is "Yes." Say no more. If a lawyer asks you if you know how much you earned last year, the correct answer is "Yes." Do not say, "Yes, I made $75,000, but I pulled in an extra $60,000 in the stock market. But I don't see what that money has to do with my spouse!" Just listen to the question and answer it concisely.
- *Be honest.* Do not spill out confessions of every wrongdoing you may have committed during your marriage (unless asked). Just

answer each question honestly and to the best of your ability. If you cannot remember the answer to a question or if you are not sure about your answer, just say what you know. Remember, you can preface your answer with, "I am not completely sure, but..." What is important is that you do not try to hide your misdeeds, because chances are the lawyer knows about them anyway, or soon will. Remember, the opposing party is well trained at spotting inconsistencies in your deposition testimony and will make you look foolish if he or she catches you in a lie. Finally, you may face perjury charges if you are caught in a lie and, perhaps even worse, the judge will question your credibility for the rest of the case.

- *Do not be self-conscious.* Assume the lawyer asking you about your personal life already knows the answer to every question. Your spouse has told his or her attorney all the intimate details of your life together. Now it is the lawyer's job to get you to admit it on the record. This can be embarrassing, but a deposition is not a press conference. The lawyers and the court reporter will not go to the local bar afterward and announce to everyone your full name and litany of marital sins.

- *Dress and behave appropriately.* A deposition is a formal proceeding. Treat it that way by dressing neatly. Do not snack or chew gum.

- *Do not joke or be sarcastic.* Remember, everything that you say will be written down by a court reporter who is in the room with you. Jokes and sarcasm may be understood in context, but they will not be reflected appropriately when the judge is looking at the written transcript of the deposition.

Attorneys are trained to do their job. They have questioned hundreds of witnesses in hundreds of depositions. The attorney has the advantage of knowing where the questioning is going and, probably, what your answer will be. Think of this like a football game: The receiver and the defender both run down the field during a passing play. The receiver has the advantage, and it is not his speed or strength. Instead, it is that he knows where the ball will be thrown. The defender must guess and react to his opponent's actions. You are the defender in this scenario, so be on your toes and try to react to your opponent instead of trying to predict what he or she will do next.

8. What will a deposition do for my case?

A deposition is a valuable tool for your attorney. It is not only used to gather facts, but it also allows your attorney to learn more about the other side's case, the personalities involved, and what tactics are likely to be used in the future. Your lawyer may learn that your spouse is highly defensive when questioned about personal finances, for example; that fact may be used during settlement negotiations or trial.

In depositions, both lawyers get a better idea of how the other side plans to testify. It helps them predict what may happen during the trial. Take this hypothetical example of Louise and Ralph. Louise suspects her husband, Ralph, had an affair with his auto mechanic, Lillian, and even spent some of the money Louise earned at the national bingo championship to buy flowers for his mistress. However, Louise does not know for sure that this happened. During the deposition, Louise's lawyer may ask Ralph where he was on the afternoon that Louise expected him to trim the shrubbery. Based on credit card statements Louise's attorney received during discovery, he may ask Ralph why he purchased a bouquet of roses from Fanny's Flower Hut on his credit card, roses that Louise did not receive. During the deposition, Ralph admits to buying the flowers and sending them to Lillian, claiming, "She just had toe surgery and you want to keep a good auto mechanic happy!" These tidbits of information may help build Louise's case against her philandering husband as the divorce process continues. However, this type of digging around for proof may not be allowed at trial, so a deposition may be just the place for such important inquiries.

Depositions also provide a good opportunity to settle a divorce case. Let us presume that Ralph spills details of his strangely close relationship with his auto mechanic. During the deposition, Ralph blurts, "She really knows how to tune up an engine!" His lawyer fears Ralph is about to admit to spending his wife's bingo money on his sparkplug-loving mistress, so they huddle up and settle. Ralph and his lawyer offer Louise a settlement that includes repayment of her bingo money. If Ralph and his attorney decide not to settle at this point, Louise has important information and admissions on the transcript to support her case once it goes to trial.

What if Louise's lawyer questions Ralph about his suspicious flower purchase and Ralph claims to have sent the roses to the local nursing home—and he claims to have proof? Louise's attorney knows that accusing Ralph of wasting their money on extramarital affairs could be a dead end. He may suggest that Louise settle now to save more legal fees, irritation, and valuable time.

Depositions can be eye-opening experiences for both you and your attorney. You may feel your lawyer does not seem as strong as your spouse's counsel or your case does not seem as strong as your spouse's case. In this sense, a deposition can be a reality check. It is like having a toothache. You cannot wait to have the painful tooth extracted, but once you enter the dentist's office and see the drills and clamps, you feel wary.

However, after the dental procedure, healing can begin—and it is the same in a divorce. You want to get out of a painful marriage and start your life anew. But once you go into a deposition and see a court reporter poised to document your admission of getting drunk and throwing ceramic pottery at your spouse's head, you think: "Do I really want all my private skeletons released from the closet and presented to the world? Do I want my children to know about all this?" You or your spouse may settle. Even if you reach a verbal agreement at this point, you have this agreement on the transcript, under oath. You can figure out the paperwork later.

Remember, it is easy to sit in your lawyer's office, discuss the case, and feel you are invincible. However, once you are face to face with your spouse and his or her attorney, you see that the other side is working just as hard as you to succeed. You also see that divorce is not a pleasant procedure. Stay calm and talk about what went on in the deposition with your lawyer afterward.

9. Who pays for the court reporter? How much does this service cost?

The party requesting the deposition pays for the associated costs. Usually, the court reporter charges $25 to $50 an hour, although fees may vary depending on where you live. Court reporting is a skilled job, and this person's accurate recording of the proceedings is very important. There is a supplemental charge if you ask the court reporter to transcribe the notes or to create an official document containing everything that was said during the deposition. If the other side wants a copy of the transcripts, they will purchase one from the court reporter. Those transcripts can be a valuable tool for your divorce and trial. Again, do not worry about the court reporter divulging your secrets to others—these are skilled professionals and they understand that the proceedings are not public. This person is present merely to record what everyone says, not to comment on it. The witness whose deposition was taken, even if it was not you or your spouse (such as a witness to adultery or even the suspected girlfriend or boyfriend), may also purchase a copy of the transcript.

10. How should I prepare for the deposition?

Beyond looking and behaving appropriately, as was discussed earlier, your attorney may suggest that you practice your answers in a mock deposition. If you are feeling nervous about the process, ask your lawyer to practice a cross-examination of your testimony. During cross-examination, the other lawyer will ask you tough questions about your own testimony. Often the opposing party will try to undermine your testimony with other evidence or try to catch you in a lie. By practicing in your attorney's office a few days before your deposition, you will be better prepared to answer the opposing attorney's questions without nervousness or trepidation.

If you can afford the extra time with your attorney, have him or her videotape your answers to the questions. This will allow you to see your body language and responses to hard questions. Watch your facial expressions when you are answering questions about difficult subjects. Some people hesitate even when answering an easy question such as "Do you know what time it is?" If you struggle to answer simple queries, then you will probably break when faced with tough ones. The more you prepare for this process, the more familiar it will seem. Familiarity breeds a more relaxed attitude.

11. What happens if I do not settle my case after the deposition?

Settlement should always be in the forefront of your mind. It is almost always better for the parties involved in a dispute to determine their own future as opposed to a judge determining it for them. However, if you do not settle after the deposition, do not fret. At the least, you and your lawyer will have a better idea of the merits of the case. At this point you can decide whether you want to spend more money to pursue the case further or try harder to settle. Usually, one side comes out looking weaker during a deposition. Something often surfaces during a deposition that weakens one side's case, even something as simple as the fact that you cannot suppress a smile when talking about a past incident. These are the little chinks in the armor that lawyers love to see in their opponent. Perhaps a disgruntled spouse seems so bitter and angry that the judge will never have sympathy for him or her.

A deposition can let you know if you need more facts or research. Perhaps the deposition makes it clear that you do not know how much you earned in a certain year and need to access your financial records or consult an accountant. Perhaps you need to consult other financial advisors to discover how pensions can be divided. Depositions give everyone a clearer notion of the case and how it will likely proceed.

If you do not settle your case, you and your attorney will prepare for a trial in a courtroom. You must prepare well for a trial because time may be limited and judges want you and your spouse to get down to business and make it easy for them to resolve the case. You will want to present your case efficiently to sway the judge to your viewpoint.

During trial preparation, your attorney may try to bypass a lengthy and expensive trial by mediating your dispute. In some jurisdictions, mediation is court mandated; however, frequently mediation is voluntarily entered into by both parties. In the next chapter, we will talk more about the mediation process and how it can help you and your spouse agree on important decisions that will affect your lives after divorce.

Chapter 4

Mediation: Reaching an Amicable Settlement Without a Judge

Always be open to the possibility of a joint settlement as an alternative to trial. Remember, going to trial is time-consuming and expensive. By going to trial you place your postdivorce life in the hands of a judge who can identify you only by a case number. You want as much control as possible in deciding what your life will look like after your divorce. Therefore, sometimes you may find it beneficial to enlist the services of a professional mediator to help you and your spouse agree. A mediator is a professional with specialized training in the art of dispute resolution. Your lawyer should help you find a good, reputable mediator in your area and assist you in determining if mediation is your best option.

1. What is mediation?

Mediation is generally an informal and voluntary process through which both parties try to reach an amicable settlement with the help of an impartial intermediary. The strength of mediation lies in the parties' ability to come to a mutually agreeable settlement, which facilitates healing and gives the parties a chance to determine their own future instead of leaving it to a judge who may not do what either of you want. Often, you and your spouse will be diametrically opposed on certain (or most) issues relating to how marital assets should be divided or the custody of your children. You both may believe compromise is impossible. Approach mediation with an open mind because, unlike a trial, it is something that you have the power to control.

2. Is a judge better prepared to resolve my dispute?

You and your spouse can come to an agreement—before, during, or after the divorce. Usually, you can agree in two basic ways. First, you can sit down with your spouse and your respective lawyers and hammer out your own agreement. Or second, you and your spouse can go to court, where you will have a trial before a judge, and in rare cases (primarily in Texas and Georgia), a jury. If a trial is needed, the judge will resolve your disputes and you will have to live with his or her decision.

The judge may not be the understanding person you imagined. He or she may not be someone who will see that you have suffered emotional pain because of your spouse's neglect. He or she may not see that your ex-spouse would be fairly served if the final result handed 50 percent of his or her lucrative business over to you. Remember, judges may be impartial, but they are extremely busy and they are human. Your judge may have his or her own problems the day your case comes up. Judges wade through thick dockets of cases. Some judges may not even be used to ruling on divorce cases. They usually take a realistic approach to divorce and are therefore more inclined to say, "Your marriage is over. You do not live together anymore. That is your reward for dealing with your spouse's conduct. Now, let's divide the assets fairly and we can all move on." Divorce is not about revenge, especially for a judge who sees hundreds, if not thousands, of cases per year. For the judge, it is about helping you get on with your life. Once the judgment is rendered and the gavel pounds, you are stuck with the ruling, so trial should be a last resort.

Everybody has a different outlook for his or her postdivorce life. For some, getting on with life depends on receiving a fair portion of the assets accumulated during the marriage. If this sounds like you, then your most important ally in obtaining that goal is you. Therefore, you must try your best to reach an amicable agreement without getting to the stage of a court trial.

3. What type of provisions can I have in a settlement agreement?

You may include any provisions you and your spouse can agree upon. The caveat to this general rule comes when children are involved. When children are at issue, a provision must be in the best interest of the child. That being said, your settlement agreement may include provisions that divide your savings, debts, and property, or even provisions for child support payments and child custody, provided the payments and custody arrangement further the best interest of the child.

4. Will the court address religion or determine in which religion my children will be raised?

Courts are very resistant to getting involved in issues such as which religion is best for a child. Parents have a right to expose their children to their own religious beliefs, within reason, and the courts will usually respect that. Whoever has legal custody of the children may decide things such as which church the child belongs to, whether the child will have a bar or bat mitzvah, or whether a child will observe Islamic, Jewish, or other dietary rules. However, most lawyers and judges will try to designate a parent as the final decision maker on those issues after the parents have consulted each other in a good-faith discussion.

Depending on your religious beliefs or values, it is also important to outline if there are any faith-related or religion-inspired actions you want in your settlement proposal and agreement. Talk with your religious or spiritual leader to be certain that you provide the supplemental language, if needed, to ensure that both parties cooperate with any religion-related procedures to effectuate a divorce within your religious beliefs.

In the Jewish religion, a "get" is required to enable the spouses to remarry under Jewish law. Because a "get" requires each of the parties to meet with an approved spiritual leader with specific certification, sign a document, pay a sum, and follow through on this action, it is often helpful to have that detailed in the settlement agreement, including a date to secure it by in order to make sure both parties cooperate. If there are other important beliefs or traditions that must be covered, discuss them with your clergy or faith-based leadership and become knowledgeable about what is required.

It is imperative to share that information with your lawyer ahead of time so it will be clearly and properly handled in writing and there will be no significant actions left unidentified that need to be completed following your divorce.

5. Who can be a mediator, and what do mediators do?

A mediator is an impartial person who will listen to both parties' grievances and postdivorce goals, weigh each party's argument, communicate each party's proposed offers and settlements, and then help the two parties agree. Stated differently, a mediator is a facilitator: he or she facilitates a resolution. The overriding purpose of mediation is to find a way to reach a binding and amicable settlement between you and your spouse.

A mediator can be anyone: an accountant, a lawyer, a priest, or a rabbi; however, my preference is for a good divorce lawyer who can provide sound judgment and a reality check when necessary. This way, if needed, the mediator can politely explain what could happen at trial given the facts of your particular case. Each community sets standards for mediator training, so your lawyer should be familiar with good mediators.

6. How much does it cost?

A good mediator will charge approximately what a good divorce lawyer will charge, and that amount varies from community to community. Ask your attorney what the prevailing rates are in your area. Mediation is often an all-day process. The fee can be split any way the parties prefer. If one person has all the money, then he or she can pay for the mediator's fee. It is, after all, marital money. Another option, which you may feel is appropriate, splits the fee because both sides are benefitting from the process. In this case, neither will prolong the mediation just to cost the other side money.

Ultimately, the judge will determine whether the agreement you reach in mediation is legal and if it is in the children's best interests. If it is, the judge will likely incorporate the agreement into your divorce decree. Regardless, judges strongly appreciate an agreement that both sides have come to on their own. Mediation is a way to help both sides meet in the middle on thorny issues; the mediator is the person who will help you get there.

7. Do some divorce lawyers specialize in mediation?

Yes. Many divorce attorneys take mediation training for this type of work. Some lawyers like to do mediation because it gives them a chance to see how other lawyers present their cases. However, one characteristic most divorce attorneys/mediators have in common is that they do it because they like to help people. Mediation helps people resolve their differences without having to go to court.

8. What does the mediation process look like as opposed to going to trial?

In mediation, both parties come together for one or a series of meetings to discuss contested issues. At the outset, the mediator will give his or her introductory remarks and try to put everyone at ease. The mediator will make certain that everyone knows you cannot use what is said in mediation later in court. Just like attorney-client privilege, discussed in Chapter 1, your communications and settlement offers are generally not admissible in court. The mediator cannot later be subpoenaed (that is, served a legally binding requirement to come to court and testify in a case). This meeting is strictly for settlement discussion. If you disclose in mediation that you have a new bank account, opposing counsel can later subpoena that bank. However, that information must be shared anyway.

After the mediator has given his or her introductions, each party (either you or your attorney) will present the case, meaning your lawyer will get an uninterrupted chance to state the facts as both of you understand them. Then the other side makes their opening statement. If things are amicable, the parties can remain in the same room to begin and sometimes complete discussing the settlement. If not, or if things get more heated, the parties will split into separate rooms. In already contentious cases, the separation of the parties can be done at the start of the process.

The mediator goes from room to room in a kind of shuttle diplomacy. That way, you can get things off your chest to a mediator that you do not feel comfortable discussing in front of your spouse. You may tell the mediator, for example, it is imperative you stay in the house and gain primary custody of the children because you think their best chance for a good education is in your school district. However, your spouse may insist his or her new condominium is in a superior school district and your children can transfer to the new school and get a better education. The mediator will go back and forth, learning more about each side's feelings on the matter to find middle ground.

After both parties have made their cases, the mediator will communicate—with each party's permission—certain information to the other party, hoping to reach agreement. A good mediator, one who specializes in divorce and who understands the implications of going to trial, can, upon request, offer informed opinions about how each party may fare at trial. The mediator may come in and say, "It looks like the most likely scenario is that the husband will pay $2,000 a month in child support if it goes to court." Or, the mediator may suggest, "What about joint custody, with the husband paying $1,000 a month in alimony and $75,000 in a lump sum settlement?" A settlement is achieved only if both parties agree to the terms.

You would be surprised how effective mediation can be, even in the toughest divorces. The power of mediation is that it is voluntary and it puts the power of settlement in the hands of the parties themselves. Before accepting any offer from the opposing party, both sides can go back to their respective corners to think about it. In the hypothetical mediation settlement offer above, the husband may want to pay less in alimony and more up front. He can either accept or reject this offer completely or he can reject part and amend part. As this chapter has clarified, the big difference between mediation and going to court is that when you go to court, the judge decides and you go home and do what the judge has ordered. In mediation, you have more control over your destiny. You make the decision and then live by it.

9. Can a judge order you to go into mediation?

Yes. The judge can order that you go to mediation. In some jurisdictions the parties must mediate during the pretrial stage. From the judge's perspective, one important reason for mediation is that it saves the judge a lot of time and effort because many of those cases settle and do not require a trial. As discussed earlier, most judges will tell you that you are better off handling your own dispute rather than letting a judge decide the outcome for you. Think about it. The judge is busy, and therefore he or she will hear from you for only a few hours and then decide things affecting the rest of your life. You know a lot more about your life—your past suffering, your futile efforts to keep your spouse solvent, or your connection to the children. You do not know this judge and you do not know what life experiences will affect his or her rulings. For example, this judge may not have lived in the same house for many years. Consequently, he or she may not think that you must get to stay in the house you built and lived in for the past 30 years. By turning to mediation, you maintain control of your agreement. Judges are happy to let you seize that control and agree to something you both can live with.

10. What are some disadvantages to mediation?

The biggest disadvantage to mediation is that the mediator's primary goal is settlement, which does not always equate to justice, particularly your view of justice. A mediator, especially one used often by the court, wants to regularly report to the judge that he or she has settled a case, taking the tough work off the judge's hands.

The mediator might favor an obstinate party. One party may come to mediation rightfully arguing he or she is entitled to $100,000 in alimony and child support—and he or she would likely be granted such relief at trial. The other party stubbornly says, "I will not give more than $10,000." It becomes the mediator's job to get a compromise that may mean getting the person willing to give $10,000 to move up to $50,000 and the person wanting $100,000 to accept $50,000. While this may seem fair at first glance, perhaps it is not actually fair for the party who would have obtained better relief in court to settle for less in mediation. Examples like this highlight the importance of having a good divorce lawyer or someone knowledgeable about divorce cases as your mediator—someone who understands divorce and who has seen these cases before. In this sense, a mediator can give a reality check to the stubborn party and may, if asked, say, "I know you guys are far apart, but I have to tell you that a judge would probably come closer to $100,000." Honest information about possible outcomes can help guide the settlement.

11. What if my spouse and I are deadlocked and cannot agree on a settlement?

A good mediator can recognize when a case cannot settle. Each side may think their argument is perfectly reasonable and would prefer to take their chances at trial rather than settle for less. Remember, you are paying not only your lawyer but also the mediator. If a settlement is unobtainable, then a good mediator may go to each side and say, "You guys are never going to settle this because you are too far apart." While it is better to settle in most cases, there are a few situations where it is better, and even cheaper, for you to go to trial.

For example, let us say that one spouse, for whatever reason, does not want a divorce. He or she might say, "I will be damned before I let my spouse get away with this! I am not letting that person take my kids out of my house!" In this type of case, it could take months to get the couple to settle. Some people just need someone in a judge's robe to tell them it is over and outline what they must do next. A good mediator will help you understand this scenario and react to it. A lawyer may not see the other side's perspective or hear the discussions, but a mediator does.

12. Where does mediation take place?

The process of mediation usually occurs in a neutral site, such as in the courthouse or in the mediator's office. The location depends on where both parties feel most comfortable. That being said, there may be a strategic—and practical—advantage to going to the opposing counsel's office. You will be a guest on his or her turf, and if you are feeling abused or you are not getting the results you expected, you always have the right to say, "That's it. We're walking out!" Conversely, you and your attorney cannot walk out of your own attorney's office.

Regardless of where you choose to meet, mediation is an entirely voluntary process and you can end it for whatever reasons you choose.

13. Can a judge change my mediated agreement?

No, a judge cannot change the agreement you reached during mediation. However, the judge can refuse to make it part of the court's order. Stated differently, your mediation agreement is not worth the paper it is written on unless the judge decides it should become part of his or her final ruling. Barring any illegality or unconscionable provisions in the agreement, the judge will likely adopt your agreement and make it part of his or her final ruling. If there is something wrong with your agreement, the judge may tell you to go back and renegotiate or go to trial. However, that is very rare.

The judge is also more likely to adopt your agreement if you were both represented by good lawyers because he or she will see that you were given good advice—or at least had the opportunity to receive good advice. The judge may question portions of your agreement that do not comport with settlement norms. For example, if your spouse is paying significantly less in child support than your state's statute requires, the judge may ask for clarification. You may have to explain that he or she will pay for the house, where the children will live, or for their private school tuition, and that these expenses were considered in determining the child support figure. You can agree to do anything that is legal.

The judge's main concern is getting you through this process and making sure you never have to return to court. The judge will look at your agreement with an eye toward clarifying any ambiguity that may cause future turmoil. If you form an agreement that says, "Husband and wife agree to agree on all major medical decisions," the judge will probably say that one party needs to have a final veto right so that if you cannot agree you will not wind up back in court, arguing about who will make the decision.

A note about settlement and pro-se (unrepresented) litigants: If you do not have a lawyer, or if you are facing a party not represented by a lawyer, the judge will likely look at the agreement very carefully to ensure that the pro-se litigant is not taken advantage of during the process or does not agree to a settlement that is unconscionable and impossible to do, which might necessitate future court involvement

lawyers and start with new ones in the event settlement efforts are unsuccessful, and while that is certainly a negative, the process also helps push spouses to continue along the settlement path and avoid the trial path. Lawyers, judges, and theorists are in and will likely remain in disagreement as to whether this process is appropriate. And not all states even permit it (although most do). Ask your lawyer about collaborative law if it interests you.

There are unfortunate times when even the best of intentions do not result in a settlement agreement. When settlement is not an option, you will be on the path to trial. In the next chapter we will discuss what you can expect if your case reaches a trial.

Chapter 5

The Trial: The Last Resort

Trial should always be the last resort. As we have discussed, divorce cases do not go to trial if other methods can be found to settle disputes and forge an agreement. Sometimes the parties cannot agree on important matters and trial is the only remaining option. This chapter will help you prepare for and understand the trial process. The courtroom is a place where you will formally dissolve your marriage and find resolution to your differences. It is not a dramatic soap opera. Instead, court is a place where you will finally get closure and consistency in your life, but it almost certainly will not give you the exact resolution you had hoped for.

1. What is the truth about divorce trials?

With the help of alternative dispute resolution techniques such as mediation, divorce trials are becoming exceedingly rare. Despite what you have seen in movies and on television shows, divorces are usually settled with the help of two lawyers and, occasionally, a mediator. The judge comes in at the end of the process to approve the agreement and make it legally binding.

If you and your spouse cannot agree—even on the last tiny point—you may have to let the judge decide. In the previous chapter, we outlined why letting the judge determine your future is not the ideal resolution for your divorce. Sadly, for some, trial may be the only way to solve a dispute. If your case ends up in court, you will have a limited amount of time to present your case to the judge, who has a busy caseload. Preparing for your court appearance is very important, and your lawyer will need a great deal of help from you to get you what you want.

2. How much does going to trial cost?

Divorce trials can be very expensive. It seldom costs less than $10,000 to $20,000 for your lawyer to prepare for and conduct a divorce trial. Costs can go even higher, up to $100,000 or more, if the issues are complex and include disputes about, for example, the value of a self-owned business or which parent gets primary custody. By the time your case goes to trial, you should have a good sense of the cost of legal proceedings, but again, it is always appropriate to ask your lawyer how much, or how much more, the case will cost. Know how much it will cost and how long it will take if you proceed to trial, and take that into consideration when analyzing a settlement.

In most states, the court can award attorney's fees to be paid by one spouse to the other. But this is up to the judge's discretion, and after a full trial between two people who once loved each other deeply, many judges wish to be done with the case and may see a request for an award of attorney's fees as furthering the litigation. Your lawyer should explain your chances of receiving an award of attorney's fees from the judge to whom your case is assigned.

3. At the outset of my representation, should I ask my lawyer about the possibility of a trial?

Yes, you must know every possible scenario that could occur in your divorce. Ask about the standards, or legal measuring sticks, for custody or child support issues that may be determined in a trial. You will more easily accept a settlement if you know what will happen if you go to trial. Knowing the likely outcome of going to court and facing a judge's decision will help you and your lawyer settle the case before the trial ever happens.

Lawyers may write a letter to the other side early on, detailing what they expect to achieve in court. On your behalf and only with your permission, they may offer to accept a settlement close to that, or even a little bit less, to save time, money, and attorney's fees. A good lawyer will put in writing only what he or she is very certain will be the outcome of the case or something close to that expectation, based on the information he or she has. If the lawyer is willing to stake his or her reputation on this estimation, based on the facts, then the offer must be close to the actual outcome he or she believes you will achieve at trial. Your attorney may be sending this letter to cover you when the discussion of who will pay attorney's fees is argued after trial. In some states, your lawyer may show this letter to the judge after the trial and final ruling and say, "All the money they spent after we sent this letter was wasted, because they could have had this same result early on if they'd only accepted the offer outlined in our letter."

Also, a good lawyer may send an offer to the other side at the beginning and then eventually achieve the same outcome through a trial; at least he or she tried to get the couple to form an agreement without the extensive time and money spent on a trial. Good lawyers and reasonable parties can then feel like they tried to save time and money but were forced to litigate. And they can save the rejected settlement offer as proof.

7. Do expert witnesses get paid for their services?

Yes, these expert witnesses are qualified professionals in their field. If you call the witness—perhaps a real estate appraiser to assess the value of the house you and your spouse are fighting over—you pay for his or her services. Such witnesses may cost thousands of dollars for their research time, preparation, and presentation of their testimony. These professionals are working for you and your case and must be paid for their time and service.

8. Should relatives and friends testify on my behalf?

It may seem counterintuitive, but it may not be in your best interest to have your family and friends testify on your behalf. Although these people can provide insight into past events and the atmosphere of your home life, your closest family and friends will be speaking from a biased opinion, and the judge is cognizant of this. It is easy for an attorney to highlight a friend's or family member's bias. The typical cross-examination of a relative goes something like this:

Opposing attorney to wife's mother: "You are testifying that your daughter was mistreated by her husband."

Wife's mother: "Yes."

Opposing attorney: "Would you say or do anything to help your daughter?"

Wife's mother: "Yes, of course I would."

And there you have it! You may also be surprised by the testimony given by your so-called trusted family member or friend. It is not uncommon for in-laws to support their son- or daughter-in-law's point of view, criticizing their own child's bad marital behavior. Be cautious when you call a close family member or friend as a witness because you cannot predict what that person will say once he or she is on the witness stand!

As you can see, trials can be risky, emotionally charged experiences. Your case is at the mercy of the judge's decisions, so it is worthwhile to prepare thoroughly with your attorney beforehand and keep your emotions in check. If you are discussing marital property—such as a house, cash, or business assets—a divorce trial can be stressful enough. But what about when children are involved? No situation is more fraught with tension. It's impossible to measure the impact of a judge's decisions concerning where your children will live, with whom they will live, where they will attend school, and other serious matters. In the next chapter, we will discuss custody and what you need to know before you fight for your vision of your children's future.

Chapter 6

Issues Related to Child Custody

Children are human beings and it is the responsibility of both parents to raise them with love, to care for their emotional, physical, and educational needs, and to make decisions about their future.

If a divorce involves no children, it should be a lot easier to reach a settlement. This is because children are the only treasures you share with your spouse that cannot be given a monetary value or split in two.

Most judges will tell you that they dread custody cases. They do not like to play God, and in many divorce custody cases, that is what they are asked to do. It is heartbreaking to see two parents fight about who will have control over their children's lives. Judges must draw from their knowledge, their past experience, the presentations of the parents and their lawyers, and recommendations from neutral experts to make these all-important decisions about the children's futures.

1. What is custody?

The term *custody* refers to a parent's legal right or obligation to house and care for his or her children and make decisions concerning their upbringing, schooling, religion, medical care, and other matters. Custody is divided into two areas: physical custody and legal custody.

We will discuss the difference between them in a moment, but first it is necessary to understand how custody decisions are made. The best custody determination occurs when both parents agree on custody without going to court. In these situations, their lawyers can draw up an agreement that outlines the framework of the custody of their children and the parents can implement it immediately. This agreement may include things such as where the children will live, how long they will spend with each parent, who will make decisions about education and medical care, and even who will pay for summer camp. The possibilities are endless, and therefore your custody agreement can be tailored to your specific facts.

Many parents cannot agree on these issues because each parent wants to play the same role in the lives of the children. As you can imagine, these issues are highly sensitive and negotiations can drag on or grind to a halt at any moment. If this occurs, the parents must go to trial and have their custody issues resolved by a judge.

2. What is physical custody?

Physical custody refers to where the children will live—their primary place of residence. It can also refer to what periods of time the children will be with each parent. Visitation (also called parenting time) is a part of physical custody. Therefore, you might have physical custody of the child, but the child visits with the other parent less than 50 percent of the time. The issue becomes, which parent is the child's primary caretaker? As a general rule, if the children are in your care for over 50 percent of the year, then you are designated the primary physical custodian.

The primary physical custodian usually makes the day-to-day decisions about the child's life. Ideally, he or she will make these decisions with input from the other parent. Perhaps there is a question of whether

Felicia can go to the park with her friends after school to play soccer. The parent with primary physical custody would probably make that decision. Unless the other parent has visitation rights, and would prefer that Felicia go ice-skating with her cousins, the first parent's decision stands because that parent is the primary physical custodian.

The parent with primary physical custody might make other, more important decisions, such as where the children go to school or camp, what extracurricular activities they may participate in, and what doctor to call when a child has an earache. Ideally, both parents will discuss these issues and agree on decisions concerning their children. If not, they will defer to the agreement provisions covered under legal custody. (See question 4.)

3. What is joint custody?

Joint custody is not as legally significant a term as you might think, although you hear it often in the news or in movies. More significant are the details, the fine print of the custody agreement. Most parents would be unconcerned with the label of *custody* if they could see their children often (perhaps Wednesday through Sunday), rather than have joint custody that translates to only one weekend a month with their children. Therefore, the details are most important. Do not get hung up on the words. Granted, joint custody may sound nice, but focus on the specifics of your agreement, such as the dates and times you will spend with your child.

4. What is legal custody?

Legal custody is another intangible concept. It means a person is given the right to make the legal decisions about the children's upbringing, such as decisions about medical care, education, and religion. Joint legal custody is emerging as a favored concept in many divorce cases. This means that parents with joint legal custody both have the right to make important decisions about school, medical care, religion, and other important issues in their children's lives and have access to their children's records.

Whether dealing with joint legal custody, sole legal custody, or primary legal custody, a good lawyer will make sure there is a provision that both parents strive to agree on these important issues. However, it is important for one parent to have primary legal custody for times when both parents cannot agree on certain issues. Since parents cannot always agree on everything, the custody agreement will name one parent as the default, the person to make the decision.

For example, Jane has primary legal custody of the children in her divorce agreement with Todd. Jane would like the children, Perry and Lisa, to attend her Methodist church's Bible camp next summer. But Todd, who is Jewish, would like to enroll the kids in a Jewish camp in the Blue Ridge Mountains. They disagree for months, but it is Jane who gets to decide the camp choice because she has primary legal custody in their agreement.

The bottom line is that any major decision about the children should be spelled out in the agreement. Who will decide? Perhaps decision making is divided, with one parent deciding medical issues and the other parent deciding educational issues. Do the parties have to go to mediation before they make the decision? Or does one person get the right to decide, period?

In some agreements, a trusted third party (such as a clergyman or respected friend) can act as a tie breaker. However, unless the parties agree to it, courts rarely allow the power of the final decision to be shifted to a third party. Judges usually may not legally order or designate psychiatrists or others to decide tough disagreements in the future. The parents have the right to decide for their children.

If they cannot agree, and if a third party has not been approved to make decisions, the judge is designated by law as the ultimate tie breaker. To avoid this situation, the court will designate a parent as the final decision maker. That parent may and sometimes should rely on expert advice, but that parent will have the ultimate right to decide the future when parties cannot agree.

As you propose an arrangement, think about what issues affect you. Do you trust your ex-spouse to make the same decisions you would about the child's religious upbringing? Do you feel strongly about what school your children attend? Perhaps you could agree, for example, that if your spouse is willing to pay the tuition, he or she is entitled to decide which private school the children attend; otherwise the children's residence determines the school district.

5. Can my spouse and I agree about custody without a lawyer?

Yes. If you and your spouse cannot fully agree about a custody arrangement or other aspects of your children's living or schooling arrangements, you can come to a partial agreement. It is best to try to agree on as many issues as you can with your spouse before trial. It will benefit both your children and yourselves not to extend a custody case any longer than it must be. Try to sit down with your spouse. Discuss the basic elements of your child's life: school, religion, camp, sports, and so on. What large holiday celebrations does your family hold each year? Should Billy spend Christmas every other year with Grandma Lucy in Atlanta and the others with Granny Theresa in Pittsburgh? Are Christmases on Mom's side of the family huge celebrations, something Billy will not want to miss? Perhaps he could spend each Christmas with Mom and each spring break with Dad on the boat in Key West.

You probably will not agree on everything. But you may continue to agree on many things you and your spouse have always agreed upon. You can also ask for help from respected members of your community, such as a clergyman. Perhaps Father John has always been a mentor to both you and your husband. If he can take an objective approach, Father John could be a big help.

6. What should I do if my spouse and I have agreed on custody?

Congratulations! Now go to your lawyer and ask him or her to immediately draft an agreement you both can sign. Even if you can only agree on certain aspects of custody, make sure that they are in writing and will be binding on your spouse should he or she renege later. For the issues on which you and your spouse do not agree, you and your lawyer will draw up a proposal to present to the judge, outlining why your plan for the children's upbringing is the right one. Your spouse will likely do the same, so be prepared to stay calm, and let your lawyer present your case well. No one can "win it all" in custody cases. The best thing you can hope for is that the children make it through this difficult time with as little disruption as possible.

7. When are custody issues usually decided?

Custody issues are decided during a divorce case regardless of whether the parents come to a settlement through depositions, mediation, and negotiation, or by going to trial in a courtroom. At other times, parents see fit to change this agreement after they are divorced. There are three different types of custody cases (for children born during marriage):

- custody decided within the context of a divorce case (while the case is ongoing or at trial);
- enforcement of custody arrangements after a divorce, when parties violate the agreement; and
- modification of custody arrangements after a divorce case by returning to court.

8. How is custody decided in a courtroom?

The judge will base his or her decision on a legal standard. This term refers to basic rules that the judge may use to help make a decision. A judge will consider many factors to determine custody. The judge must determine what is in the best interest of the child. It may seem obvious what the best interest of the child is; however, it is one of the simplest, yet most vague standards in the law. It is almost always better to resolve custody between you and your spouse than to leave it in the hands of a judge.

9. What is the lawyer's role in litigating custody disputes?

The lawyer's role in a custody case is to present a complete picture to the judge of what it would be like if the judge granted custody to his or her client. This does not mean the attorney's client is a superior parent or has a lot of money. Instead, the lawyer will stress that his or her client can provide the child a warm, safe, loving, and healthy environment in which the child can prosper. Perhaps the best indicator of this is the client's past history of taking good care of the child. In some circumstances, the lawyer may need to impeach the other parent's character to prove his or her client is better suited to have custody of the children.

10. What is a guardian ad litem?

Many courts appoint a third party—often an attorney—to represent the interests of the children, whose interests otherwise would remain unrepresented in a custody dispute. After all, it is the children who are affected most by custody determinations, not the parents. The guardian ad litem helps the judge determine what decision would be best for the children. In this respect, the guardian ad litem is a hybrid of a lawyer and a witness. Some states consider this person more of a witness, while others view him or her more as a lawyer. Either way, a guardian ad litem is appointed to help look after the best interests of the children.

The guardian ad litem's role is to investigate a situation and make a recommendation to the court as to what would be best for the children. A guardian ad litem may interview the parents, friends, teachers, and anyone else who may have insight into the children's day-to-day upbringing. As you can imagine, the guardian ad litem obtains a wealth of information, and his or her opinion affects the judge's assessment.

Guardian ad litems cannot make everybody happy. That is not their job. Their role is to give an honest opinion to the judge and to be a representative for the children, or at least for the children's interests. Picture yourself in a courtroom. Mom is wearing her pink Sunday church dress. Dad is wearing his new three-piece suit. They both say, "Judge, look how presentable we are. We both want custody of our children." The judge acknowledges that they look well dressed and presentable and both have good lawyers. However, he or she cannot see what it is like behind the scenes; this is where the guardian ad litem's investigatory findings and insight are invaluable.

In this respect, the concept of a guardian ad litem goes against much of what lawyers learn in school. This role requires the lawyer to act as a witness who often bases his or her opinion on hearsay (out-of-court statements about a topic). In most court cases, testimony based on hearsay is inadmissible because the original person providing the information, such as the teacher or neighbor, is not there to be cross-examined by the lawyers. The wealth of a guardian ad litem's findings must be weighed against the negative implications of admitting hearsay; the judge almost always rules in favor of admitting the guardian ad litem's testimony.

A guardian ad litem can also help by giving you a better idea of what will happen in court once he or she has finished his or her investigation. If the guardian will recommend that your spouse get custody, maybe you can cut a better deal before you get to court. You can negotiate for more time with your child on the weekends or holiday trips. If you know, for example, that the guardian will recommend that Mom get primary custody—and that Dad see the child every other weekend—perhaps Mom can base her request for child support on that arrangement.

11. What is the judge's role in litigating custody disputes?

The judge's role, as discussed at the beginning of the chapter, is very difficult. He or she must decide the fate of a child. The judge must assess the parenting skills of both parties and what type of home and upbringing each will provide. The judge must also determine the needs of the particular child or children. One of the hardest needs for a child to meet is the need to be with both parents. Most judges would like to see that in the months leading up to the divorce, the parents have been willing to involve each other in decisions about the children. Although they will be divorced and living separate lives after this trial, they must work together to raise their children in this new and awkward arrangement.

12. Is there a presumption that one parent is better than the other?

No. There is not a presumption that one parent is better for the child than the other parent. Determinations of child custody are extremely fact specific. The judge should not presume that mothers make better parents than fathers (although judges are human beings and some have their own biases). Despite the commonly held misconception that there are laws favoring mothers' rights to custody, more and more fathers are being awarded primary physical custody of their children when the judge believes it will be best for the children. This may result from more women becoming the primary breadwinner while more men are becoming stay-at-home dads. But do not be frightened. Each case is judged on its own merits and circumstances.

Across the United States, more parents are being granted joint custody, or shared responsibility for their children. In some states, such as Florida, the presumption is that it is better for parents to have shared custody. In other states, the court does not have that presumption, but judges must look at the option of joint custody. The national trend is for judges to consider joint custody or shared parenting responsibilities in almost all divorce cases.

13. Do wealthier parents usually win custody?

As this chapter has stressed, there are no presumptions in child custody and determining what is in the best interest of the child. One parent's ability to provide a fancier house or more toys should not sway a judge in a custody case. It is entirely possible for a father to provide a warm, loving, clean, and stable home in a double-wide mobile home. Perhaps he works nearby at a construction site and spends a great deal of time with his son, playing ball and providing for his day-to-day needs. The mother may offer a mansion for the child, with every kind of electronic gadget and a state-of-the-art computer system. However, she is always away on business trips. When she is home, she is constantly on the phone making business deals. She pays little attention to her child. She figures her son would rather play on the Internet anyway. There is no substitute for good parenting! The judge will likely opt to place the child with the father in the trailer park.

Having familial support for your parenting, such as having relatives nearby, can sway a judge. Support systems are important. If the mother has her parents living within a few blocks and the father wants to live on an isolated ranch in Alaska, the judge may decide in favor of the mother, even though it is not fair to the father, because it is probably better for the child to be in a familial environment. Remember, when at all possible, structure is very important for children.

Judges want to know that parents will try to normalize their children's lives. Judges appreciate parents who can sit down with each other to discuss their custody issues. While you may be angry with your spouse, minimizing how your feelings trickle down to your children is vital. If the judge can see how you set aside your frustrations with your spouse for the sake of the children, you will be ahead of most divorcing parents.

14. How should I behave in front of the judge?

The judge will use many tools to assess the matter before him or her. He or she may rely on the parents' testimonies. He or she may rely heavily on the testimony of an outside observer, such as a psychologist. The judge may even speak with the children themselves to find out what situation would be best for them.

The judge will not want to see two vicious parents using their children as weapons in their attacks against each other. He or she will not like hearing evidence of a mother saying, "I'm going to make sure you never see the kids because of your cheating!" Instead, the judge would like to see this mother, although angry at her ex-husband for cheating on her, still make sure that he gets to see the children every other weekend and other times in between. Unfortunately, it does not go without saying that parents must put their children's needs first and not use them in their battle against their spouse.

To help you prove to the judge you can act in a mature manner (and help yourself), consider enrolling in a parenting course for divorcing couples. While there, you may learn new approaches to ordinary problems and discuss your new role in this changing family landscape. The court will likely make you enroll in such a course anyway, so you look mature and wise to the judge if you have already done so without being ordered.

15. Is it common to seek counseling or psychiatric help during a custody case?

Counseling is helpful in most divorce cases, especially those where the two parties are making difficult, emotional decisions concerning their children. If someone is having a hard time with the process, judges usually prefer that he or she seek help independently, without court intervention. Going through counseling voluntarily adds another layer of structure and stability. Few judges will think, "She must have problems because she is seeing a therapist." More likely, judges will think, "If I were going through this, I would need a psychologist too."

16. Is a psychological or custody evaluation necessary?

If you find you and your spouse cannot agree on a custody arrangement either through mediation or through direct dialogue, the court may order a custody evaluation. A custody evaluation is a process through which a psychologist or social worker examines all parties involved in the custody dispute—parents and kids—and makes a recommendation to the court about what he or she thinks will be in the best interest of the child. As part of the evaluation, the psychologist may have the parents submit to psychological testing and make assessments based on the results. You should be informed of the psychologist's findings before the court is made privy to them. If the information is favorable to your side, the custody evaluation can be a substantial bargaining tool. However, if the custody evaluation is not favorable to you, then perhaps it is time for you and your attorney to consider settlement.

The judge will take the psychologist's recommendations seriously and will often abide by them. Consequently, as this book has tried to stress, it is in your best interest to settle as many issues as possible without court intervention. There is a strong advantage to you and your spouse settling your disputes on your own terms, as the two of you understand your situation better than a judge could, and you will ultimately be the parties living with the outcome.

17. Is there such a thing as a standard custody arrangement?

No. We all hear about one parent having custody and not the other and how one parent sees the children on holidays and every other weekend. However, most judges would rather have the parties work out what is best for their family. A custody arrangement is not the end of a relationship; instead, it is a blueprint for the future of your children. Nothing is guaranteed and everything is negotiable in such cases. Often one parent will be the primary custodian, with the child living at the home and spending time with the other parent. But the specifics can vary as much as human beings can.

The majority of custody agreements split weekends equally between parents and then divide midweek and holiday visits. If Easter celebrations are very important gatherings in your family, for example, then you might have your child be with you for that holiday each year. However, you may have to make some sacrifices in order to compromise. Ideally, a custody agreement will be drawn up and then locked in a drawer until there is a problem. If a time comes that the two of you stop cooperating, then you can pull your agreement out and say, "We already agreed on me having Jimmy until 6 p.m. on Sundays."

Judges are human, and they will base their determinations on the law and past experience. A judge may have presided over an ugly case in the past in which a father tried to argue for custody by painting the mother and her family as religious fanatics, although they were actually respectable Quakers. He may not be sympathetic to your assertions that your spouse is a religious extremist who should not have primary custody. You may believe your spouse is extreme, but the judge may not see it your way.

Do not depend on the judge to make all the decisions about your children's future. It is your family. Try to work with your spouse to make your own decisions. Lawyers, clergymen, counselors, and mediators can help, but it is your decision to make. When your case and the marriage are completely over, you still must work together to make many decisions about your children. More information on a parenting plan is supplied in the Resources section and can also be accessed online at www.ksfamilylaw.com/FAQS/parent _planscheduling.

18. Can we modify our custody agreement after the trial?

Yes. However, there are some state-specific restrictions. Often parents find it necessary to return to court after their initial trial to revisit the agreement and seek a new arrangement. To make a dramatic change in custody—to transfer the primary place of residence from one parent to the other parent, or from a parent to another relative—you almost always need a major change in circumstances. This change must be based on more than just problems, such as the child having bad grades one semester or a parent being injured in an automobile accident and not being able to pick up the child at day care. You need something significant, such as one parent being arrested for driving under the influence or using drugs. Some states, however, allow you to return to court and argue that the current arrangement is no longer in the best interests of the children. However, custody is not easily modifiable; therefore, you had better make sure that modification is necessary before you invest significant time and money in another trial. If you and your former spouse can agree to a change, you can do it informally, or you can formalize it through a new court order. A court order is usually best.

19. What happens if my spouse or I want to relocate?

Relocation is one of the most common reasons for a postdivorce change in custody. In many states there are laws providing that when a parent relocates, it may be necessary to revisit the custody arrangement. We have a constitutional right to live where we want and have our children come with us. However, these constitutional considerations must be balanced with the best interest of the child in mind. Maybe the child is happy and successful in his or her school, and a move that is based solely on spite could ruin that situation. A judge may not side with the relocating party.

Sometimes a change of custody is necessary. Let us presume that 14-year-old David has been living with his mother in New York City, where she is an actress on a soap opera. His father lives in a small town in Montana. David loves his high school, is a junior varsity basketball star, and has many friends. However, the mother's role on the television show was just canceled. She needs a job, so she takes a position as an entertainer on a cruise ship line, which means she will be sailing for months. There is no school on the ship for David, but she wants to keep her son, so she offers to homeschool him. David does not like the idea, and neither does David's father. He takes the mother back to court, and the judge draws up a new custody arrangement under which David will spend the school year with his father in Montana and summers on the ship with his mother. Although it is not the perfect situation for David, it is the best situation the family can arrange.

20. What are the standards used by judges in a change-of-custody or postdivorce custody case?

During the divorce the main custody standard is "What is best for the child?" In a change-of-custody case, the standard varies from state to state but is often "What is now best for the child, and has there been a significant enough change to justify modification?" This standard is sometimes hard to satisfy.

The judge must usually decide whether circumstances have changed so much that a change must be made. Therefore, there is a much heavier burden of proof on the person seeking modification to show why such a change is warranted. It is even more important for you to prove your case if you are seeking a change. Do not go back to court because you did not like the first judge and want to try your luck on another one. The trend nationwide is for your case to go back to the same judge. Judges do not like to change their minds and may become angry with people who keep coming back to court instead of working issues out on their own. Also, this is not an appeal of the original decision. Your case cannot be based on the assertion that the judge did not understand the facts the first time.

Sometimes circumstances change and a new custody arrangement becomes necessary. It may be due to adverse conditions in the child's primary place of residence, such as excessive fighting with the parent or a stepparent. Or, it may be due to a child's needs changing as he or she ages, such as when a child has exceptional athletic or artistic talent and may benefit from moving to a different location for special schooling or training.

21. Is a change in custody worth it?

A change-of-custody battle can be as expensive as a divorce and just as emotionally draining. That being said, unlike most issues, custody cannot be quantified. You can decide who gets the cars and the house, but custody disputes are very expensive and difficult. How can you put a price on an extra week with your child? Many people will sacrifice future earnings for custody. Parents will give up the opportunity to take a lucrative job if it means they can have their children live with them.

Changing custody is very difficult, and a change should be based on only very serious problems or needs. It is probably not worth your time, money, and emotional well-being to get an additional day with your child each month or to get $50 more per month in child support. However, this is a choice you must make for yourself after discussing the details with a lawyer.

22. Can remarriage affect my custody agreement enough that my ex-spouse can seek a modification?

Remarriage alone may or may not be a significant enough change in circumstance to justify a change in custody. However, new spouses can either complicate or enhance a custody situation. A new spouse who is a good person and nurturing to the children can be good for the children. Children want their parents to be happy and to have loving relationships. However, if a stepparent or new boyfriend or girlfriend is doing something bad, such as abusing drugs or alcohol or hitting or sexually abusing a child, then this situation can be grounds for a change, or even for filing a separate, criminal charge. Perhaps a new stepparent does not want to be an instant parent and does not want to have the child living in the house. Both parents could either come up with a new agreement with their lawyers or, if they cannot agree, go back to court to hammer out new details of their arrangement.

Sometimes, the stepparent is the best role model for the child. The following is a true case: A divorced father was in prison, but was married to a stable woman. While the father was in prison, the mother filed for change of custody. The mother, however, was itinerant and could not hold a job or provide a stable home for the child. Thankfully, the father's new wife was a terrific parent. The judge awarded custody to the jailed father, so in effect, the stepmother would be taking care of the child.

23. Can a child tell the judge what he or she wants?

Yes, often. However, this rule varies from state to state, and it depends on the age of the child as well. In most situations the older the child, the more likely the court will be to listen to and follow his or her wishes.

Courts vary on whether they will listen to a young child. A guardian ad litem or an appointed psychologist can listen to the child and then report to the judge. However, judges do not want to burden the child by making him or her choose between parents, which often leads to parents bribing their child with goodies. Maybe Mom will not let her child have his or her own cell phone or stay out until 2 a.m. on Saturday nights. Therefore, Dad tells the child, "Live with me and you can do whatever you want! I'll get you your own cell phone and a new car, too!" The judge will frown upon such bribery.

24. What if one of the parents violates the custody agreement?

Minor violations should be worked out between you and your ex-spouse. Perhaps you can turn to a counselor or mediator if it becomes a source of constant disagreement. However, when the situation becomes unbearable or when one parent violates the agreement in a major way, it may be necessary to return to court to enforce the agreement.

Most judges abhor petty visitation disputes. Remember, the child is an innocent victim in this situation, and parents should act like parents, not like children. Let us presume you are a divorced mother. You recently met someone and you have a first date with the new guy on Saturday night. Dad tells you on Friday night that he is not picking up the kids on Saturday afternoon for his visitation time because he does not want to. He seems spiteful, as if he is backing out of his obligation on purpose to mess up your social life. He does it repeatedly, often asking the children when Mommy has a date. This is the type of situation that a judge would prefer the parties work out themselves.

If this type of behavior is occurring, it is in your best interest to document the incidents and confront your ex-spouse about why this is happening. Maybe you can preempt these problems by having a babysitter clause that requires the ex-husband to pay extra child support to cover babysitting costs if he cancels a visit. Or perhaps you could work certain penalties into the agreement if one party does not uphold his or her obligations. Or you could even have a backup plan for yourself. Pay a babysitter, and after the fifth or sixth time, return to court and ask for reimbursement for the babysitter. You may even choose to keep paying a babysitter rather than a lawyer since another court case is the last thing you want to get into. Remember, you can avoid litigation headaches later by preventing problems in the initial agreement. But if your efforts fail, you can ask the court to assist you.

25. When do you go to court over violations of the agreement?

Bring a violation to the court's attention only when it becomes worth it to pay a lawyer. Make sure you are above reproach. You do not want to accuse your ex-spouse of something if you are guilty of other serious breaches of the agreement.

Enforcement is a tough issue, and you need to put as many mechanisms into the final agreement as possible to avoid this battle. A provision might state that no parent may deny visitation rights to the other without going through a counselor or mediation or he or she will incur a financial penalty. The overall theme to this chapter: People can agree on anything, as long as they agree. In daily life, working together to raise children is imperative.

Sometimes it is necessary to go back to court to enforce the agreement with the power of a judge's order. If one parent repeatedly disappears for weeks and is not there to take care of the child at his or her appointed time, it may be necessary to go back to court to enforce or even change the agreement. Or, if one parent attempts to take the children to a new home and bar the other parent from his or her visitation rights, it may be necessary to go back to court to enforce the agreement. Cases such as these can be difficult to try because specific facts and evidence must be proved, and sometimes there aren't easy legal solutions.

26. What if one spouse is from a different country and wants to take the children there?

International custody issues can be even more of a nightmare. They do arise, as portrayed in the film *Not Without My Daughter*, based on the true story of Betty Mahmoody. In this situation, Mahmoody's Iranian-born husband took the family to visit Iran and then refused to leave. Iranian laws protected the father's right to keep his daughter in Iran and raise her as a Muslim. Mahmoody's American citizenship could not help her in such a situation. If you and your children are caught up in an international custody dispute, time is of the essence—and be prepared for a long and hard battle.

Custody or visitation issues involving parents from different countries can often be complex and difficult. If this is the case in your situation, consult immediately with an attorney familiar with these specific issues. If you or your spouse is from another country, or if there is some reason to fear your child will be taken to another country with or without your permission, act quickly. An initial suggestion is to secure your child's passport and put it in a place where your spouse could not possibly obtain it. If your child does not have a passport, obtain one for him or her and then secure the passport. Check out the information on the U.S. State Department's website at www.travel.state.gov/abduction/abduction_580.html regarding international custody issues.

Obviously, the most important thing is to exercise common sense if you are fearful that a parent or anyone else is trying to take a child out of the country. If you can stop it, do not let your child leave the country until you have spoken with a lawyer versed in this area. If you have reason to fear your child will be taken and not returned, immediately seek legal protection, hire a lawyer, and seek an emergency order. Most important, do not let the other parent have the child if there is a fear that the child will be taken to another country; explain that you will not return the child until you get good legal advice.

In today's world, children have family in other countries and it is not suggested that they should never be allowed to visit with relatives outside of the United States. However, if there is a real threat of children being taken and not returned, the best thing you can do is to become knowledgeable about this issue. There are international laws to help retrieve children after they have been taken, such as the Hague Convention on the Civil Aspects of International Child Abduction, but an ounce of prevention is always worth a pound of cure, especially in this type of situation. Not all countries have these laws, and many do not apply them as we would like.

Chapter 7

Child Support

The divorce process can be a long, arduous, and often very painful experience for everyone involved. This is especially true when the parties have a minor child or children. While no divorce is the same as any other, if a child is involved they all have one common thread—the child is the innocent party and should have the right to maintain as normal of a life as possible after the separation of his or her parents. To attain this goal, every state requires parents to support their children with both monetary and physical care. Traditionally, the duty of monetary support rested primarily on the father, while the duty of care was placed on the mother. Today, however, the duties of support and care rest on both parents.

1. What is child support?

Child support is a payment of money from one parent to another for the support of their children. Each state has its own specific guidelines for determining which parent will pay (usually the non-custodial parent) and how much he or she will be obligated to pay. In any divorce involving minor children, the parties will be required to disclose their financial status. The court will determine how much each party will pay based on that and other information. The parent with the child support obligation will pay on a monthly or bimonthly basis. If one parent fails to pay, the other parent has a legally enforceable judgment against the nonpaying parent that he or she can use to obtain a wage assignment (garnishment) or sometimes even have the nonpaying parent put in jail for failure to pay. However, it is important to note that if one parent fails to pay support, the other parent should not withhold visitation. Instead, that parent should seek court involvement or other collection measures. The nonpaying parent can be jailed for an indefinite period of time for his or her failure to pay child support, often until the full or partial amount is paid. However, if you withhold visitation (called self-help), then you may well also be put in jail—not just your nonpaying former spouse!

2. Who must pay child support?

Parents have a duty to support their offspring unless the child is emancipated, the parent or child dies, or the child reaches the age of majority, which is usually somewhere between 18 and 21 in most states. Parents cannot contract away their obligation to financially support their child because the right of support belongs to the child, not the parent. All states, however, allow parents to contract for a specific amount of child support if the contract is not against public policy or state statute (law) and is in the best interest of the child. In almost every case, the parent who has the children less than 50 percent of the time will pay child support. There are exceptions, such as when there is almost a 50/50 division of parenting time and the parents earn almost the same or when the parent with a little more time earns a lot more money.

Persons who are not biological or adoptive parents are ordinarily under no duty to pay child support. Stepparents and grandparents have no duty to pay support for their stepchildren or grandchildren, respectively, unless they have created a loco parentis relationship or have adopted the child as their own. *Loco parentis* is a Latin term that means "in place of the parent." For stepparents or grandparents, establishing such a relationship requires more than allowing a child to live with them or exercising temporary custody. Instead, courts will consider the relationship between the stepparent or grandparent and the child and determine whether the former has taken on the historical position of a biological parent. Whether a loco parentis relationship exists is a question of fact for the judge to decide, but it is very rare.

3. How do courts determine how much a parent must pay in child support?

Unlike most areas of law, family law is extremely intuitive and practical. All states require the divorcing spouses to follow child support guidelines, a formulaic calculation that weighs numerous factors relating to the needs and expenses of the child. Although the states have discretion regarding what factors may be considered, courts will look at (1) the needs of the child, (2) the standard of living established by the parents, (3) each parent's income and overall financial situation, (4) the earning capacity of both parents, and (5) the age of the child. This list is not exhaustive, and the judge may look at several other factors. Each state has its own specific guidelines.

4. What constitutes income for purposes of child support?

The following is a list of several sources of revenue that most courts consider to be income to determine child support:

- Hourly wages and salaries (including tips and overtime)
- Alimony payments
- Stock dividends
- Royalties
- Income from rental properties
- Social Security benefits
- Pension and retirement plan benefits, military and unemploy-
  ment benefits, government subsidies, gifts and prizes, and trust
  disbursements

5. Is it true that men always pay child support?

Historically, men were the breadwinners of their families. Consequently, they were tacitly assigned the duty of paying child support.
However, with the influx of women into the workforce—a direct
result of the women's movement beginning in the 1960s—courts
now take a gender-neutral stance regarding who must pay child support. Section 309 of the Uniform Marriage and Divorce Act (UMDA),
a guidepost that many states have adopted and modified to make
their own, gives trial courts discretion to order one or both parents
to pay an amount reasonable or necessary for the child's support.
Today, typically the noncustodial parent (the parent who does not
have physical custody of the child) must pay child support to the
custodial parent.

Consider this example: Jack and Jill have one child, Timmy. Jack
works at a local restaurant making minimum wage while he goes to
school at night. Jill just finished her medical residency and makes
over $200,000 per year as an emergency room doctor. Given her
long hours during school and now in the hospital, her relationship
with Timmy is distant. Compounding the issue, Jill has taken illegal
stimulants to help her with her long hours, and she has used these

drugs in front of Timmy. Jack filed for divorce and was awarded custody of Timmy. Consequently, Jill will be required to pay child support to Jack.

6. When does child support end?

In most states, there are basic circumstances that will end a parent's duty to support the child: the child is emancipated by the court, finishes high school, marries, or enters the armed forces; the parent or child dies; or the child reaches the age of majority.

Emancipation and reversion

Emancipation is a legal proceeding through which a minor child becomes legally independent of his or her parents. The child becomes fully responsible for his or her own actions. A court will look to the child's own actions to determine whether he or she should be emancipated. Marriage, joining the military, and other acts of independence will typically terminate the parent-child relationship. If a child is emancipated, the parents' child support obligations cease. However, even if the child acts independently of his or her parents, if there is a showing of need, then the child will not be emancipated or, if he or she has been emancipated, his or her status as a dependent will revert.

Death of the parent or child

If the obligated parent or the child dies—without specific language in the final court order to the contrary—the deceased parent is no longer obligated to support his or her child. Additionally, a trial court will not involuntarily extend the child support obligation of the deceased parent (or his or her estate) without express agreement of the deceased parent prior to death. Parents should (and are often required to) maintain life insurance to provide for the child after the parent's death.

Age of majority

In most states, a child support obligation ends when the child reaches somewhere between the ages of 18 and 21 years old. In a majority of states, parents cannot be forced to support their child through college. Some states, however, may require a noncustodial parent to support his or her child's college education if the parent has the earning capacity or income to enable him or her to do so without undue hardship. Despite the majority rule (that support ends at the age of majority), the divorcing parents can agree to support a child beyond the age of majority in their settlement agreement.

7. Should I be aware of any tax implications?

Yes. First, if you have the child for greater than half of the year (182.5 days), then you are the custodial parent and you may likely claim the child as a dependent on your tax return unless you and your ex-spouse agree otherwise or unless your court permits the secondary custodian to claim the tax benefits. Consult with a certified public accountant or other tax expert for this and all tax-related issues. Second, child support payments are not deductible by the obligated parent, nor are they included in the receiving parent's income (the opposite is true for some forms of alimony). Finally, if the custodial parent pays more than half of the costs of maintaining the household, then he or she may qualify as the head of household for tax advantages. However, these general rules are void if the parents file jointly. Stated differently, to take advantage of these tax benefits, the parents may wish to file individually. Consult with and rely upon a tax expert, as most lawyers, including this author, are not tax experts.

8. Can I modify a child support obligation?

In many states you can modify the child support you owe or to which you are entitled upon showing a change in financial circumstances or demonstrating that the needs of the child have changed. There are many legal avenues available for parties whose ex-spouse fails to pay support. Parents who fail to pay their child support obligation may be jailed until they pay their support, and/or their paychecks may be garnished. But what happens when you genuinely cannot pay the amount mandated by the court? Suppose you were a wealthy doctor with a successful medical practice. At the time of your divorce you grossed approximately one million dollars per year. You now have an obligation to pay $5,000 per month in child support. You were recently in a car accident and broke your back. As you have been unable to work for the past six months, your once-successful practice is now struggling to stay afloat. What options do you have? Can you petition the court to modify your child support obligation? Maybe, but in most states you must show the court that you have experienced a substantial change in financial circumstances to justify the requested modification.

9. What constitutes a substantial change in financial circumstances?

While every state has its own statutory language, what is consistent among them is that there are rules governing the modification of support that often require a party to show a substantial change in financial circumstances or the needs of the child.

Change in financial circumstances of either parent— downward modification

The majority of child support modifications occur when there has been a financial change in the circumstances of the obligated parent. Typically the obligated parent has experienced a financial hardship and is seeking a downward modification (wanting to pay less per month). This is especially true in times such as the recent past, when the United States faced some of the worst economic conditions since the Great Depression. Many obligated parents saw a significant decrease in income. But what must someone show to obtain a downward modification? Every state has its own guidelines, and therefore you should contact an attorney familiar with the specific requirements in your state. The party must show either that he or she has little or no earning capacity or that the amount he or she must pay is (or will create) an economic hardship. What is considered an economic hardship is a question for the judge and requires a close look at the obligated parent's financial situation. And, if the recipient of support has a significant increase in income or financial status, that may also serve as a basis for a modification.

Change in financial circumstances of either parent— upward modification

As previously mentioned, the custodial parent may seek an increase in child support if the financial circumstances of the obligated parent improve (or perhaps if the recipient's income decreases). Perhaps you were a new law school graduate who had just landed your first job. You had well over $100,000 in school loans and made approximately $80,000 per year. You and your spouse had one minor child together. The stresses of your school loans looming over your head and the demands of work took their toll on your marriage. You divorced and were obligated by the court to pay $500 in child support per month. Every child support payment was made on time and you never missed a payment. Being a young entrepreneur, you opened your own firm, and after a hard couple of years you are finally making money—a lot of money! Can your ex-spouse petition the court to increase your child support payments? If so, what must he or she show to succeed?

Upward modification of child support, like downward modification, is fact specific. An important factor is the increased income of the obligated parent. However, an increase in income of the obligated parent, standing alone, may not be adequate to successfully petition the court for upward modification. Besides an increase in the obligated parent's income, the court will also look at the child's needs, increased living expenses, medical and educational needs, and past and current lifestyle. But if the recipient of support has a significant decrease in income or financial status, that may also serve as a basis for a modification.

Change in circumstances of the child justifying modification

A change in the financial circumstances of a parent is not the only reason for seeking modification. Another common reason for an increase in child support is that the needs of the child have changed. The reasons for a change in the child's needs are infinite, but they may be related to an illness, disability, or educational expenses. But the change usually must be one that was not foreseeable or anticipated—for instance, the child simply growing older and needing bigger, more expensive clothes would not qualify, because that is foreseeable and expected.

10. If I file for bankruptcy, will my back child support obligations be discharged?

No. Although some debts are dischargeable (legally releasing you from liability) at the end of a bankruptcy case, domestic support obligations are one of the exceptions to this rule. See Bankruptcy Code 11 U.S.C. § 532(a)(5). Therefore, if you file for bankruptcy, your child support obligation and most alimony obligations will remain after other debts have been discharged.

Child support is only one of many domestic support obligations that a party may be required to pay. In the next chapter we will look closely at alimony, how to determine how much you may be obligated to pay or receive, some tax implications, and how long you can expect to pay or receive alimony.

Chapter 8

Alimony

Perhaps no other legal concept in this book will generate stronger emotions than alimony. The notion that alimony is an unfair vestige of a bygone era is woven into our social consciousness. Who pays it? How much? What should you know when you enter into the discussion of alimony? How should you estimate what you should receive? Who decides what you should get, if anything? And lastly, how long should you receive it if you are awarded alimony?

The common stereotype that men always pay inflated alimony awards and that women squander their support on frivolous vanities helps fuel the stigma that alimony is unjust. For you, this common misconception will only exacerbate the fighting that will occur when it comes time to determine alimony in your divorce case. In this chapter, you will gain a better understanding of the process for determining alimony and learn how to use that knowledge to your advantage if you must pay (or receive) it.

1. Is there a difference between alimony, spousal support, and maintenance?

No. You may hear your attorney use these terms interchangeably because they are all ways of describing the same legal concept.

(c) the standard of living established during the marriage;

(d) the duration of the marriage;

(e) the age and emotional condition of the spouse seeking alimony;

(f) the ability of the spouse paying alimony to simultaneously meet the needs of both spouses; and

(g) fault (not all states).

Let's look at an example: Jonathan and Melissa have been married for 18 years. Jonathan has been earning more than $200,000 a year for the last ten years and Melissa was a secretary earning $30,000 a year until she had her child 10 years ago. Since that time, she has been a stay-at-home mother. Based on the factors mentioned above, the court will likely recognize that this is a long-term marriage and it will take Melissa a few years to get back into the workforce. Because of the duration of the marriage, Jonathan will likely be ordered to pay alimony for at least a few years so Melissa can get back into the workforce. Many other factors would be relevant, including the other financial resources of the parties and perhaps fault. But the bottom line is that alimony will be determined on a case-by-case basis except in a few states where there are guidelines to give the judge some direction. Again, discuss this with a lawyer in your particular jurisdiction.

4. Can infidelity affect my right to alimony?

In some states the court will consider infidelity when it is determining whether to grant alimony. In a minority of states, infidelity that causes the divorce is a complete bar to alimony. Stated differently, if you are seeking alimony and your infidelity caused the marriage to dissolve, then you may be barred from receiving alimony. The best option is to not cheat on your spouse. But, if you have cheated on your spouse, you should never withhold this information from your attorney or the court, as lying about it may be viewed as worse than the adultery itself.

A note on forgiving cheating and its effect on alimony: If you cheated on your spouse in the past and then your spouse subsequently forgave your transgression and resumed the relationship with you, that past instance (or instances) of cheating will be less likely to be used against you. The cheating must usually be the cause of the divorce, and if your spouse has forgiven you, he or she cannot turn around and claim that your cheating caused the divorce. Whether your spouse forgave you depends on the specific facts of your case.

Your spouse's infidelity that caused the divorce will not result in you receiving more alimony. However, judges in some states may consider your spouse's infidelity when deciding alimony or when it comes time to divide the marital property. Division of property is at the judge's discretion, and there are many factors he or she may consider when it comes time to divide your marital estate. Some judges may consider infidelity and/or other transgressions that caused the divorce when they are dividing your estate, although some states require an equal division regardless of adultery or other conduct.

5. Will moving in with my new boyfriend/girlfriend or remarrying affect my alimony award?

In many states a periodic alimony award may be modified if the recipient has a meretricious relationship with a third party. A meretricious relationship is a relationship that has the trappings of a marriage without the legal effect. The relationship usually must be continuous, and the receiving ex-spouse and third party must hold themselves out to the public as a couple for this claim to succeed. Intermittent sexual relations with a third party will not be grounds for modifying your alimony obligation. If you live with someone but refrain from marriage just to keep getting alimony, the court will often see through such a ruse.

Remarriage is usually a termination point for periodic alimony, though some states permit judges to order, or parties to agree, that alimony will continue even beyond the recipient's remarriage.

6. What is the difference between periodic alimony and lump sum alimony?

Provisions requiring periodic or lump sum alimony look very similar, but one major difference between them is that lump sum alimony is nonmodifiable in most states.

Periodic alimony is defined as payments to be paid for a certain period of time or until an event, the timing of which is yet unknown. Usually the unknown timing is the remarriage or death of one of the spouses. For example, a court order may require you to pay (or receive) $500 per month in periodic alimony for the next 12 months, totaling $6,000. This number may change if the receiving spouse is in a meretricious relationship, if one spouse dies, or if the receiving spouse experiences a change in financial circumstances. Stated differently, many unknown contingencies may cause the obligated spouse to pay less than the total $6,000. A periodic alimony award can become nonmodifiable if agreed upon in the parties' settlement agreement, but absent the parties' agreement, most courts cannot make it nonmodifiable. Periodic alimony is also the only form of alimony that might be tax deductible to the payor and taxable to the recipient.

A lump sum alimony award will state the exact amount of payments due and the exact amount of each payment. The provision should state that this alimony payment is meant to be lump sum alimony and therefore nonmodifiable. Do not be fooled by the name— lump sum alimony does not necessarily require payment in one large sum, although nine times out of ten, an award of lump sum alimony is a one-time payment. However, lump sum alimony could require monthly payments over a duration, just like periodic alimony. The difference is that it is not modifiable and (unlike periodic alimony) is not deductible to the payer. Consider the periodic alimony example above: Instead of paying $500 per month for 12 months, totaling $6,000, a lump sum award may require you to make a one-time payment of $6,000 or it may require you to pay $2,000 every four months on a predetermined day over one year. Regardless, the obligated party will be required to pay the total amount ($6,000) regardless of whether one party dies, the receiving spouse is in a meretricious relationship, or either party's financial situation changes. Know that if you are ordered to pay lump sum alimony and you die, your estate may be required to continue paying until the alimony award is satisfied.

7. Can my child support obligation or our division-of-property agreement be rolled into my alimony payment?

No. Alimony is completely separate from your child support obligation and the court-ordered division of property.

8. Prior to marriage and/or divorce, can my spouse and I contract away our right to alimony in the event we get divorced? What is a prenuptial agreement?

Yes, prior to marriage you and your spouse can contract away your right to spousal support if you divorce. This is sometimes done in what is commonly known as a prenuptial agreement. To be enforceable, a prenuptial agreement usually must be (1) made with no duress or coercion, (2) made with full financial disclosure from both parties, (3) entered into knowingly by both parties, and (4) not "unconscionable." However, in most states, you may also enter into a contract after you are married but before divorce. This is commonly known as a postnuptial agreement. To be enforceable, a postnuptial agreement must meet the same requirements as a prenuptial agreement. Regardless of when you enter into a prenuptial or postnuptial agreement, most jurisdictions will enforce the contract if the rules are followed. But again, please check with a lawyer in your area, as some states do not allow postnuptial agreements and the rules for prenuptial agreements vary from state to state.

In addition to predetermining alimony, a prenuptial agreement can predetermine property division, as we will discuss in the next chapter. However, prenuptial and postnuptial agreements cannot resolve child-related issues such as child support, custody, or visitation. Those issues must be resolved based on the circumstances that exist at the time of the divorce rather than at the time of the prenuptial agreement.

Chapter 9

Division of Property: Who Gets What and Why?

If child custody is the most contentious issue in a divorce, then division of property often comes in a close second. This is the time in your divorce when the judge (via court order) or the parties (via settlement agreement) decide who will get the house, cars, boat, dogs, computers, furniture, and everything else you and your spouse acquired during the marriage. Know that there are limitations to what can be divided depending on your jurisdiction. Every court will answer two preliminary questions: (1) What property is subject to division? and (2) How much of that property should each spouse receive?

Before proceeding, note that as in every other aspect of your divorce, you and your spouse have the full power and opportunity to enter into a mutual agreement stipulating how your property will be divided. And also as with every other aspect of your divorce, you and your spouse are best positioned to make decisions about dividing your assets (and debts) because they are the accumulation of a lifetime together. You will almost always be better served by entering into a mutually agreeable settlement instead of submitting to a judge's ruling after a day or more of trial.

1. What property is subject to division?

There are different division-of-property systems in the United States, including equitable division, marital property, and community property. A majority of states use a hybrid equitable/marital division-of-property system in which property is subject to division only if it was acquired during the marriage, leaving the judge discretion to equitably (fairly) divide such property. Under this system, property brought into the marriage or received via gifts or inheritance is not subject to division unless it is comingled with marital property or the gift was to benefit both spouses at the time of transfer. Consider this example: John and Kathy just closed on their first home as husband and wife. To help the newlyweds, John's parents gave them a gift of $15,000 to go toward the down payment. This gift benefitted both John and Kathy, and therefore John cannot claim this as separate property when it comes time to divide their assets upon divorce. However, suppose the gift was intended to be given to John and not Kathy, and at the time of transfer John put it into its own interest-bearing account separate from any marital funds. During their marriage the funds were never comingled. Would those funds be marital property and subject to division or separate property? They would probably be his separate property.

Some states use what is commonly referred to as a community property system. Under a community property system, all property owned or acquired by either spouse during the marriage is subject to division. Like in marital property states, gifts and property brought into the marriage that were not comingled remain separate property and are not subject to division. The major difference between the equitable/marital system and a community property system is that in the latter, the judge has no discretion when it comes time to divide the marital assets. Once the judge decides what property is marital property, the estate will be divided equally (50/50), not equitably.

Consider this example: Mark and Stephanie have been married for 20 years. Although they started out with little, Stephanie has risen in the ranks of her company to become CEO. Their marital estate is worth $10,000,000. Mark quit working early in the marriage to take care of their children. Unfortunately, with Stephanie working long hours, Mark felt lonely. He cheated on Stephanie, causing their divorce. How will a community property state divide the $10,000,000 in marital assets? The estate will be divided equally, with Stephanie receiving $5,000,000 and Mark receiving $5,000,000.

As with all issues, ask your lawyer which form of property division your state follows and the specific rules regarding same.

2. What factors will the judge use to equitably divide my marital estate?

If you do not live in a community property state, then the judge will have discretion regarding how the estate will be divided. The judge will consider what is equitable given the facts of your case. At the outset, equitable division does not mean equal division. The judge will consider numerous factors when he or she divvies up the marital estate, and the order may favor one party over the other, meaning that party receives over 50 percent of the estate. If you are in a community property state, equity, as the term is used in an equitable/marital property system, is not a factor because the estate will be statutorily divided 50/50.

The court will look at, among other factors, (1) the length of the marriage, (2) prenuptial or postnuptial agreements between the parties, (3) the age of the parties, (4) the health of each party, (5) the occupation of each party, (6) other sources of income available to each party and each party's employability, (7) the needs of each party, and (8) the contributions of one spouse to the family unit as a homemaker. As you may have realized, the previously discussed alimony factors are similar to the factors to be considered before an equitable division of property can be made. Perhaps you have been married to your spouse for 30 years. Your spouse is a successful executive who makes over one million dollars per year and you have not worked since getting married. You have neither vocational skills nor the capacity to find meaningful employment. You take care of your son who suffered a stroke and cannot function independently. Your house is equipped to care for your son's needs. Should you be granted the marital home when it comes time to divide the estate? Most attorneys and judges would say yes. Given your lack of income, your spouse could also be required to pay the mortgage on the house as alimony.

3. Will infidelity affect my share of divided property?

Adultery is not a significant factor when dividing property in an equitable division system, and it is usually not considered in a community property system. You may remember, however, that in some states adultery is a bar to alimony or may affect property division. That being said, in a majority of states the judge decides what is equitable, which may include consideration of your (or your spouse's) adultery when dividing your marital estate. If your state permits, your lawyer may argue for—but not rely upon—adultery as a ground for receiving a greater or lesser portion of the marital estate.

4. What happens if one spouse is spending a lot of money prior to the divorce being final?

Although marital fault is becoming less of a factor for many judges, economic fault remains very important when dividing your assets.

Dissipation is the legal term used to characterize an intentional or negligent misuse of marital funds after the breakdown of the marriage or for a nonmarital purpose during the marriage. If one spouse has been dissipating marital funds, the court may well offset the property division in favor of the other spouse to compensate for the money that would have been awarded but for the dissipation. For example, Mark and Heather live in an equitable/marital property state. They have been married for ten years and had saved $300,000; if this were divided equitably at divorce, each would likely receive $150,000. However, when she saw divorce was imminent, Heather went on a shopping spree with $200,000 of the marital assets, buying clothes and cars, going on cruises, and spending money on her new boyfriend. When it comes time to divide the property, Mark will likely be awarded the remaining $100,000 and perhaps a greater percentage of the sale of the marital home, if it is sold, or other assets. Heather may even have to return some of the $200,000.

5. What other factors may the judge consider in court?

It is important to stress the intangible factors that a judge will consider. Always be on your best behavior while in court and in the days and months leading up to court. When in front of the judge, if you are a man, wear a suit or a shirt, slacks, and a tie. If you are a woman, wear a dress, skirt, or a suit. Do not be afraid to ask your attorney what he or she considers appropriate attire.

Additionally, avoid personal and emotionally charged attacks on your spouse and his or her counsel. Also be aware of your body language while in front of a judge. Do not slouch in your chair or roll your eyes whenever the opposing attorney or your spouse makes a comment. A cool and collected litigant will often reap the rewards of his or her composure, especially in the face of an angry spouse. Above all, address the court and the judge with politeness and deference. Remember, judges are human and despite any other factors, they will look favorably on people who show respect for the court.

The court may also consider the testimony of expert financial witnesses, CPAs, or forensic accountants. Even business valuation experts can be hired to make it easier for the court to decide such issues as how much property exists and whether it should be considered separate. If there are enough assets to warrant hiring such an expert, consider it.

6. How will the court treat comingled property in marital property states?

Know that separate property can become marital property, subject to division, but marital property usually cannot become separate property except where the intent to give property to the other spouse is clear. This concept is transmutation or comingling. Stated differently, if you comingle separate property with marital property, then it becomes marital property, subject to division. Whether separate property has been comingled is often a very confusing and hotly contested issue in deciding the division of property. This makes perfect sense because the person arguing against comingling wants to keep his or her property, while the person arguing for comingled property wants a bigger marital estate and a bigger cut.

Consider this example: Before your marriage you owned a home you inherited from your parents, who inherited it from their parents, and so on. After your wedding your husband moved into the home and made needed repairs to the now-100-year-old home. Over the next 30 years, you and your husband added two additional rooms to make room for your two children, and you used marital funds for maintenance and necessary repairs. Will the court consider this separate property since the home has been in your family for 100 years and you brought it into the marriage? Or will it be marital property subject to equitable division? The answer is uncertain.

7. What effect does a prenuptial agreement have on division of property?

An enforceable prenuptial or postnuptial agreement will override the division-of-property system in your jurisdiction. As mentioned before, to be enforceable, a prenuptial or postnuptial agreement must (1) not be unconscionable, (2) have full financial disclosure between both parties, and (3) be voluntary. Remember, state laws vary, so rely on the advice of your attorney. If your prenuptial or postnuptial agreement is legally enforceable, then you can stipulate your own terms for property division. If you live in an equitable division-of-property state, your prenuptial agreement may stipulate that all marital assets will be divided equally (50/50). This effectively takes the discretion out of the hands of the judge. Conversely, if you live in a community property state, your prenuptial agreement may state that one spouse will receive more or less than the other spouse at divorce. Again, despite the default rules in your jurisdiction to the contrary, you may modify or override those rules in a prenuptial or postnuptial agreement.

8. How are items other than property, such as items that were purchased together on a honeymoon, divided?

We all have numerous items of property. Lawyers and judges hate to divide the minor things such as pots and pans. You and your spouse should divide these. If you can, think of an easy way to do it, such as deciding by a coin toss or holding a garage sale. Or, get a relative or friend to help you. You can start by making a list of every item of property, perhaps in spreadsheet form. Then, next to it, indicate why you believe it is yours or your spouse's; in another column, list the approximate value; and in another column, indicate who should receive it. It is not worth the money you would spend on lawyers to divide these items, so try to do it yourselves.

Other items of property you might not think of as property could include patents, intellectual property, files including information, photographs, and anything that is not a fixture. You may also want to decide who receives certain bank accounts based on who has the better relationship with the bank and have the other person bank elsewhere to make things cleaner.

9. How is custody of pets usually decided?

Pets are considered property. They are not children and the court is not vested with the authority to award visitation with a pet (although there are anecdotes of judges doing so). The rules of division of property apply equally to furniture and pets. If a pet was adopted before the marriage, it is premarital. Otherwise, the court must decide which spouse gets to keep the pet. Please try your best to avoid leaving such a decision to a judge. You know your pets best and you really know which spouse they would be better off with.

10. What problems might I encounter when executing the court-ordered division of property and other issues?

The judge has ruled on every issue in your case, including custody of your children, alimony, and division of property. Now what should you do? Hopefully, your settlement agreement and/or the court order give you specific guidelines to follow. You may be required to sell the marital property and split the proceeds 50/50. This seems simple enough—but is it? Consider what steps you must take to sell the property and what problems may arise. For starters, you need to hire a real estate agent—but what if your spouse does not want to hire your real estate agent, preferring to choose his or her own? What if you want to sell the house for $500,000 but your spouse thinks the house is worth $600,000—who gets the final say as to what the listing price will be? After the house is sold, how soon must you pay your ex-spouse his or her 50 percent? How will you pay it?

The procedure for separating your assets can be long and tedious, and often leads to disagreements. Your attorney must make provisions in your settlement agreement (if you have one) or request that the court provide for every contingency after your divorce. If you can account for every procedural problem that may arise after your divorce, then you will be better prepared to resolve these issues. Many of these provisions can be found in form books such as the Georgia Library of Family Law Forms, available at http://www .lawjournalpress.com/player/Book_158_Library_of_Georgia_Family _Law_Forms.html, which provides forms for divorces in Georgia. This form book is intended for lawyers to use, but it may help explain what actions or motions are available to you and your lawyer. Also, a simple checklist of items to consider covering in your settlement agreement is in the Resources section at the end of this book.

Where property division is concerned, you and your former spouse will need to know that a court order requiring the two of you to divvy up your property can be contentious and may devolve into arguments over procedure. There may also be difficulties enforcing the support and visitation arrangements, but once you have a comprehensive divorce decree setting forth those obligations and rights, enforcement is much easier. Contempt of court, or the threat of contempt, will often resolve these issues.

Conclusion

In summary, I hope that *Divorce: Protect Yourself, Your Kids, and Your Future* has assisted you in understanding the process of divorce and the often complicated and confusing turns of your potential personal journey. As you face the winding road of divorce, leave no stone unturned. Explore all of your options, as you can never be too informed and knowledgeable, and depend on an experienced and competent team to assist you. Stay focused, get the facts you need, and seek the professionals who will guide and assist you through the process. And, at every step of the way, keep hope in your heart and the determination required to get through this difficult experience in a meaningful way.

On a positive and hopeful note, time and time again, years after a divorce someone who had one of the most difficult divorces you could ever imagine has resiliently rebuilt his or her life and discovered a new world filled with happiness and joy—and that could be you and your family. Good luck, and hopefully you too will find the kind of life and relationship you so richly deserve.

Acknowledgments

Valerie and Jolie, my wife and daughter, without whom there would be no point in living this wonderful and blessed life.

Marvin Solomiany, the partner any lawyer—or anyone—would be lucky to have.

Robert Miller, who worked hard on this book as a young law clerk and then lawyer in our firm.

Nancy Miller, no relation to Robert, who has been by my side as a paralegal, assistant, dear friend, supporter, therapist, and every other title that connotes encouragement and care ever since she joined my fledgling law firm in 1991.

Robyn Spizman, who has guided me in writing this book and given invaluable advice and encouragement along the way.

Jan Schroder, who has edited this book and made it much easier to read.

Susan Bernstein, with whom I started on this project over ten years ago. She helped tremendously and got the first bulk of information out of me, which has now been revised, added to, and edited many times. Without her, this project would never have gotten off the ground.

Alvaro A. Arauz, for reviewing this book and offering invaluable advice on it.

My parents and stepparents, Stan and Ellen Kessler and Janet and Victor Brown, each of whom has helped me become who I am. My dad and mom raised me with so much love that I never for a minute had any doubt that I was loved and cherished. I can only hope to be as good a parent to my own daughter. My stepparents have been in my life a long time too, and each has given me invaluable advice over the years that has helped shape who I am.

My brother, Cory, who has given me that competitive spirit (it happens when your younger brother finally beats you at one-on-one basketball in the driveway).

And finally, my two best friends, who try their best to keep me humble, Andy Burger and Ron Aviram. They are constant companions whom I have shared my life journey with. I wouldn't have it any other way.

Suggested Information Contained in a Domestic Relations Financial Affidavit

Case Information

- Affiant's name and date of birth
- Opposing party's name and date of birth
- Date of marriage
- Date of separation
- Children's names
- Children's dates of birth

Affiant's Gross Monthly Income (Yearly and Monthly)

Additional sources of income such as bonuses, commissions, overtime, business income, disability, unemployment, workman's comp, pensions, retirement, social security benefits, other spousal or child support, rental income, interest and dividends, etc.

Amounts Withheld from Monthly Gross Income

FICA, federal and state tax, insurance (medical, dental, life, etc.), Medicare tax, retirement, etc.

Assets
Checking and savings account balances, stocks, bonds, CDs, money markets, real estate equity, automobile equity, retirement, furniture, art, jewelry, collectibles, etc.

Average Monthly Expenses
Mortgage/rent, property taxes, homeowners' association dues, insurance, electricity, water, garbage, sewer, gas, telephone, mobile phone, security system, repairs and maintenance, lawn care, pest control, cable TV, Internet, housekeeper, postage, linens, groceries, meals outside the home, lunch money, household and personal supplies, clothing, grooming, dry cleaning, prescriptions, gifts, entertainment, accountant, sports equipment and lessons, vacations, pets, publications, club dues, religious and charity contributions, etc.

Insurance
Life, medical, dental, disability, homeowners/renters, automobile, personal liability, etc.

Vehicle
Car payment, gas, oil, repairs, auto tags and license, parking fees, etc.

Children's Expenses
Child care, school expenses, uniforms, private lessons/tutoring, lunch money, allowance, clothing, psychiatric/psychological counseling, prescriptions, grooming, entertainment, summer camps, sports/extracurricular activities, toys, etc.

Payments to Creditors
Credit cards, student loans, home equity loans, personal loans, etc.

For a sample form, visit www.ksfamilylaw.com/resources
_forms.php.

Key Issues in Separation or Divorce Agreements

Custody/Visitation—Minor Children

1. Type of custody arrangement

(A) Sole custody

- One parent has complete physical custody of the child.
- That parent makes all major and minor decisions regarding the child.
- The other parent may have visitation with the child, depending on the court's decision regarding the best interest of the child.

(B) Joint custody

Some families choose a joint custody arrangement to fit their circumstances. This may involve joint physical custody, joint legal custody, or both.

- Joint physical custody—Both parents have equitable rights to visit with the child. They may decide, for example, that the child will spend one week with Mom and one week with Dad, or they may decide that the child will live with Mom during the week and with Dad on the weekends.
- Joint legal custody—Both parents have equitable rights to make decisions for the child. For example, the parents may agree that

Dad will make decisions when the child is visiting with him and Mom will make decisions when the child is living with her.

2. How decisions are made with joint custody

- The parents may agree (or the court may order) that in the event that the parents cannot make a mutual decision, one parent will have final decision-making authority.
- Sometimes the parents will allocate decision-making authority based on the subject. They may agree, for example, that Mom will have final decision-making authority on educational issues and Dad will have final decision-making authority on medical issues.
- The parents will agree about how much time the child spends with each parent and on what days.

3. Who spends time with the child on special occasions

- Holidays include spring break, Memorial Day, Mother's Day, Father's Day, July Fourth, Labor Day, Thanksgiving, winter break, religious holidays, and so on.
- Special occasions include the birthdays of each parent and the child.
- Transportation, times of visitation, the child's school schedule, and costs must be considered.
- Summers:
  - Parents may agree that each will make summer plans and submit them to the other parent by a certain deadline so that both may make plans accordingly.
  - Parents may make a summer schedule to fit their lifestyles. They may need to make child care arrangements, especially for summer, or allocate a few weeks to each parent of uninterrupted parenting time.

- Weekends:
  - When does the weekend begin? For example, is it Friday afternoon, when school ends, or Saturday morning?
  - Transportation and methods of communication must be addressed.
- Weekdays:
  - If one parent has the child during the week, the other parent may wish to spend time with the child during the week besides his or her weekend visitation.
  - Parents will want to consider which day or days the non-custodial parent will visit with the child and settle issues of times, locations, transportation, and so on.

4. Parental relocation
If one parent moves, will that parent pay for visitation with the child (e.g., airfare)?

5. Third-party rights
Sometimes a third party may wish to have some rights regarding your child. The child's grandparents may wish to have visitation, for example, or if your spouse is not the child's biological or adoptive parent, he or she may try to obtain some rights to stay involved with your child.

Child Support
Depending on the state, child support may be calculated by using an automated worksheet that considers each parent's monthly income. You will need to decide what amount of child support is sufficient to ensure your child's needs are met. This depends on a number of factors, including, but not limited to, how much time you will be spending with the child, your income, the child's expenses, and so on.

1. Other issues regarding child support
- Date of payment
- Form of payment
- Number of payments (e.g., once per month, twice per month, etc.)

2. Modification
- Child support may be increased, decreased, or terminated due to several circumstances.
- Some common situations when modification is appropriate include the following:
  - The obligor suffers a loss of or decrease in income.
  - The obligee remarries or has an increase in income.
  - The child turns age 18.

3. Education expenses
- Parents are not obligated to support their children beyond a certain time (such as age 18, depending on the state).
- Some parents wish to make an agreement regarding the child's educational expenses, especially in cases where the parents plan to send the child to college or private school.
- Some issues to consider:
  - Maximum amount each parent will pay for educational expenses
  - Maximum time that each parent will pay for educational expenses
  - Conditions upon which a parent will cease paying for the child's education, such as the child dropping out of college or moving from a private school to a public school

Tax Exemptions for Dependent Children

Who will claim the children as dependents on his or her income tax returns?

Medical Insurance

- Depending on the parents' incomes and who maintains health insurance for the children (if at all), the parties may agree for (or the court may order) one parent to provide health insurance for the children.
- Health expenses may include medical, dental, vision, psychological, and so on.
- Financial considerations include monthly premiums, annual deductibles, and amounts not covered by insurance (e.g., is the medical plan an HMO or PPO, or are only specific providers covered?).
- COBRA coverage must also be considered.

Spousal Support

Sometimes the parties may agree to or the court may award spousal support. If you wish to seek spousal support or you feel you may be obligated to pay spousal support, the following issues may arise:

- The incomes of both spouses
- Duration of spousal support
- Dates, amounts, and form of payment

Property

In some states, property may be classified into two groups:

- **Marital property**—This is property obtained during the marriage or as a joint effort of the parties during marriage. Some examples include the marital residence (or a value thereof), cars, vacation homes, furniture, joint bank accounts, and so on.
- **Separate property**—This is property belonging to one spouse only, such as property obtained prior to the marriage or property inherited or received as a gift by one spouse.

Income Tax

Some income tax issues include:

- Refunds due
- Amounts owed
- Back taxes owed
- Whether to file jointly or separately during the year of divorce

Sometimes parties may seek indemnification from any outstanding tax liability.

Miscellaneous Issues

- Current or anticipated lawsuits—that is, potential monies coming in and/or potential monies owed
- Wills
- Division of other assets, such as stock options, business interests, retirement plans
- Division of family-owned businesses
- Social Security ten-year marriage rule (discuss with your attorney)
- Attorney, guardian ad litem, psychologist, mediation, and other fees of divorce and custody litigation
- Mutual release or stipulations for right to modify or go back to court—for example, will modification be preceded by mediation unless there is an emergency?

The Parenting Plan

What is a parenting plan?

A parenting plan, also sometimes known as a parenting schedule, is a proposal submitted to the court by each parent that outlines which days each parent will have with the child. When the custody of any child is at issue between the parents, each parent will prepare a parenting plan or the parties may jointly submit a parenting plan. It will then be up to the judge to decide where the child goes and for how long. The final decree in any legal action involving the custody of a child must include a parenting plan.

How does a parenting plan/schedule work?

There are many ways to arrange a child visitation schedule. For example, if one parent has primary physical custody, the other parent may get the child every other weekend, every other holiday, and for a few weeks during the summer.

What if my spouse and I cannot agree on a parenting plan?

If you and your spouse cannot agree on a permanent parenting plan, then each of you should prepare a proposed parenting plan on or before the date set by the judge. It will then be up to the judge to decide which plan is in the best interest of the child.

What should I include in the parenting plan?

The following are the areas that should be covered in your parenting plan:

- **Details of the parenting plan.** Indicate whether the parenting plan is new or modifies an existing parenting plan and whether the parties agreed to the terms of the new plan or it was implemented by a judge.
- **Child(ren)'s information.** State the child(ren)'s names and dates of birth.
- **Custody and decision making.** State whether custody and decision making are to be with the mother, with the father, or joint.
- **Primary physical custodian.** State who will be the primary physical custodian for each child and who will make day-to-day decisions, major decisions (about educational and nonemergency health care, religious issues, and extracurricular activities), and how disagreements regarding these decisions will be resolved.
- **Parenting time/visitation schedules.** Detail parenting time schedules, including weekdays, weekends, major holidays (Thanksgiving, winter break), spring, summer, and fall vacation, other holidays (Martin Luther King Day, President's Day, Mother's Day, Father's Day, Memorial Day, Fourth of July, Labor Day), the child(ren)'s birthdays, the parents' birthdays, any religious holidays, and so on.
- **Start and end dates and times for parenting time.** State what day and time parenting time starts and ends and detail transportation arrangements for this.
- **Contact during parenting time.** Give information for the noncustodial parent to contact the child(ren) (and vice versa) when the child(ren) is with the other parent.
- **Supervision.** Indicate whether parenting time is supervised or unsupervised, and if supervised, who the supervisor will be and which parent will be responsible for the cost of it.

- **Communication provisions.** Include language regarding notification to the other parent if one parent changes residences or phone numbers.
- **Access to records and information.** Include language allowing both parents to have full access to the child(ren)'s records relating to school, health, religious, extracurricular activities, and so on.
- **Parties' consent.** Initial each page and sign the parenting plan on the last page, indicating both parents are in agreement to the terms of the parenting plan.

For a sample form, visit www.ksfamilylaw.com/resources_forms.php.

Index

KESSLER & SOLOMIANY
FAMILY LAW ATTORNEYS

http://www.ksfamilylaw.com